Oxford Discover

Student Book 4

Kathleen Kampa

Charles Vilina

OXFORD
UNIVERSITY PRESS

Scope and Sequence

UNIT	READING	VOCABULARY	GRAMMAR
▶ **BIG QUESTION 1**		**Where are we in the universe?** Science: Astronomy	
1 Page 6	**Bella's Home** Science Fiction **Reading Strategy** Visualizing Changes	**Reading Text Words** moon, asteroid, comet, meteorite, solar system, stars, galaxy, universe, spacecraft, telescope, observatory **Words in Context** vast, dwelled, speck, disk **Word Study** Words with ei	**Predictions with Will** Future statements I will visit those places again, Bella thought.
2 Page 16	**Traveling Together Around the Sun** Science Article (Nonfiction) **Reading Strategy** Compare and Contrast in Science	**Reading Text Words** astronomer, space probe, core, gravity, orbit, matter, distance, diameter, surface, craters, unique **Words in Context** bodies, explore, inner, outer **Word Study** Words with the suffixes -ance and -ant	**Future Real Conditional** Future statements and questions If technology continues to grow, we will travel to these places ourselves.
▶ **BIG QUESTION 2**		**How do we know what happened long ago?** Social Studies: Histor	
3 Page 26	**Hidden Army: Clay Soldiers of Ancient China** Magazine Article (Nonfiction) **Reading Strategy** Author's Purpose	**Reading Text Words** army, soldiers, uniform, emperor, armor, treasure, archaeologist, tomb, jade, clay, peasant **Words in Context** battle, generals, varnish, coffin **Word Study** Words with the suffix -ist	**Verbs Followed by Infinitives** Simple present and simple past statements and questions The Chinese government plans to keep it closed for n
4 Page 36	**Stumbling upon the Past** Realistic Fiction **Reading Strategy** Predictions	**Reading Text Words** dinosaur, skull, ravine, examine, discover, excavate, layers, paleontologist, ash, sedimentary rock, pastime **Words in Context** favorite, dream, tripped, determine **Word Study** Words with ie	**Verbs Followed by Gerunds** Simple present and simple past statements and questions Javier enjoyed playing with his friends.
▶ **BIG QUESTION 3**		**Where does our food come from?** Social Studies: Geography	
5 Page 46	**The Breakfast Quest** Humorous Fiction **Reading Strategy** Conclusions	**Reading Text Words** sugar cane, wheat, cinnamon, butter, vanilla, ingredients, bark, plantation, steamship, spoil, leopard **Words in Context** gather, introduce, peel, coax **Word Study** Phrasal verbs with drop	**Present Continuous for Future Plans** Present continuous statements and questions I'm making a special breakfast today.
6 Page 56	**From the World to Your Table** Informational Text (Nonfiction) **Reading Strategy** Summarize	**Reading Text Words** convenient, export, local, process, package, farmer's market, agriculture, corporate farm, decrease, century, chemical **Words in Context** grocery stores, food labels, organic food, whole food **Word Study** Four-syllable words	**Polite Offers** Simple present questions and answers Would you like to know where your food comes from.
▶ **BIG QUESTION 4**		**Why do we make art?** Art	
7 Page 66	**Art Through New Eyes** Magazine Article (Nonfiction) **Reading Strategy** Text Features	**Reading Text Words** sketch, pastels, canvas, paintbrushes, shapes, string, three-dimensional, prodigy, street painter, carpenter, sculptor **Words in Context** complex, washable, combines, fascination **Word Study** Words with the prefix dis-	**Indefinite Pronouns** Simple present and simple past statements and questions I want to paint something in this room.
8 Page 76	**Sketches in a Gallery** Realistic Fiction **Reading Strategy** Value Judgments	**Reading Text Words** exhibition, frame, landscape, texture, shading, perspective, contrast, space, stained, brilliant, pale **Words in Context** ignore, worries, famous, speechless **Word Study** Synonyms	**Offers with Shall and Will** Future statements and questions "Shall I show you some more sketches?" he asks.

Jay

Meg

Harry

Anna

LISTENING	SPEAKING	WRITING	WRAP UP

Looking at the Stars
A conversation about stars in a galaxy
Listening Strategy
Listening for reasons

The Speed of Light
A science report about how fast light travels
Listening Strategy
Listening for main idea and numbers

Talking About Differences
The first picture has a quarter moon.

Asking About Quantity
How much water is on Jupiter?

Writing Complete Sentences
The Earth revolves around the sun.
Writing Practice Write about an object in the universe (Workbook)

Choice Questions
Is Ganymede a planet or a moon?
Writing Practice Write about exploring the universe (WB)

- **Writing**
  Write a compare and contrast report (WB)
- **Project**
  Create a model
- **Review**
  Units 1 and 2 (WB)
  Big Question 1 Review

An Ancient Town
Children discuss a very old town
Listening Strategy
Listening for similarities and differences

A Nigerian Myth
A myth about the sun and the moon
Listening Strategy
Listening for gist and sequence

Giving Reasons
I'd like to go back to an ancient Maya city.
I want to see how Maya people made pyramids.

Describing with the Senses
What did dinosaurs sound like?
They probably sounded very loud.

Verb Tenses
The first emperor died when he was 49 years old.
Writing Practice Write about something that happened long ago (WB)

Count and Noncount Nouns
A lot of volcanic ash was above the bone.
Writing Practice Write about something old that people might look for in the ground (WB)

- **Writing**
  Write a descriptive report (WB)
- **Project**
  Create a time capsule
- **Review**
  Units 3 and 4 (WB)
  Big Question 2 Review

Where My Food Comes From
A girl explains the types of food she eats
Listening Strategy
Listening for examples and numbers

Types of Farms
Reporters discuss types of farms
Listening Strategy
Listening for reasons

Giving a Reason for a Preference
I like oranges, but I prefer bananas because they are easier to peel.

Talking About Food in Your Area
People often grow apples where I live.

Interesting Adjectives
My chickens lay wonderful eggs.
Writing Practice Write about a delicious meal (WB)

Prepositional Phrases of Location
The asparagus is near the carrots.
Writing Practice Write about a real or imaginary garden (WB)

- **Writing**
  Write a research report (WB)
- **Project**
  Create a story
- **Review**
  Units 5 and 6 (WB)
  Big Question 3 Review

Art Around the World
Children discuss art they like to make
Listening Strategy
Listening for reasons

An Important Painting
A tour guide discusses a famous painting
Listening Strategy
Listening for differences and details

Talking About a Picture
What are the children doing?
They're painting.

Expressing a Desire or Wish
I wish I could paint like Claude Monet.

Compound Predicate
Picasso painted many masterpieces and created many sculptures.
Writing Practice Write about a work of art (WB)

The Articles A/An and The
Theo went to see an exhibition.
Theo went to see the exhibition of Zayan Khan's landscapes.
Writing Practice Write about an artist (WB)

- **Writing**
  Write an opinion essay (WB)
- **Project**
  Act in a play
- **Review**
  Units 7 and 8 (WB)
  Big Question 4 Review

LISTENING	SPEAKING	WRITING	WRAP UP

Cities and Water
The reasons why many cities form near bodies of water

Listening Strategy
Listening for reasons

Giving Reasons
My city grew because it is next to a river.
The river was important because people used the water in many ways.

Capitalize the Names of Bodies of Water
River Seine, Lake Texcoco, Pacific Ocean

Writing Practice Write about a city near water (WB)

- **Writing**
  Write a persuasive essay (WB)
- **Project**
  Create a travel brochure
- **Review**
  Units 9 and 10 (WB)
  Big Question 5 Review

Benefits of Cities
Children share what they like about the cities they live in

Listening Strategy
Listening for facts and opinions

Asking Questions with *Have To*
Do people in your city have to recycle bottles and cans?

Coordinating Conjunctions: *And, But, Or*
I play chess with my mother but not with my father.

Writing Practice Write about parts of a city (WB)

Public Service Announcement
An announcement on how to stay healthy

Listening Strategy
Listening for advice

Asking and Answering Personal Questions
What do you do when you catch a cold?
I drink a lot of water and sleep as much as I can.

Give Advice with Commands
Eat healthy food every day.

Writing Practice Write about good health habits (WB)

- **Writing**
  Write an interview (WB)
- **Project**
  Conduct an interview
- **Review**
  Units 11 and 12 (WB)
  Big Question 6 Review

The Body's Bones
Facts about the bones in the human body

Listening Strategy
Listening for who's speaking and details

Explanations with *That* or *Where*
What is the stomach?
It's a part of your body that breaks down food.

Subject/Verb Agreement with Indefinite Pronouns
When everyone works together, you can do great things!

Writing Practice Write about exercise (WB)

Creating a Blog
An explanation of how to create a blog

Listening Strategy
Listening for gist and details

Giving Examples
My dad gets news from the newspaper.

Pronouns
When early humans discovered how to make fire, they told their friends.

Writing Practice Write about how news travels (WB)

- **Writing**
  Write a news story (WB)
- **Project**
  Create a school news program
- **Review**
  Units 13 and 14 (WB)
  Big Question 7 Review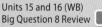

School News
A school news program for students

Listening Strategy
Listening for facts and opinions

Giving Opinions
I don't think that all blogs are interesting because some are boring.

Regular and Irregular Verbs in the Present Perfect
George has learned a lot from this science blog.
I've seen the inside of a television studio.

Writing Practice Write about a mass media job (WB)

Earthquake Preparation
An explanation of how to prepare for an earthquake

Listening Strategy
Listening for problems and solutions; main idea and details

Possibilities
There might be a lot of rain.

Contractions in Present Perfect Sentences
We've bought extra water in case of a storm.

Writing Practice Write about a force of nature (WB)

- **Writing**
  Write a how-to speech (WB)
- **Project**
  Create an emergency poster
- **Review**
  Units 15 and 16 (WB)
  Big Question 8 Review

Weather Warnings
Reporters give extreme weather warnings

Listening Strategy
Listening for recommendations

Talking About Needs
We need to get water bottles.

Adverbs of Manner
The waves were violent. They smashed violently into the hotel.

Writing Practice Write about an imaginary, dangerous situation (WB)

Food Chains
Children explain desert food chains

Listening Strategy
Listening for sequence

Describing a Sequence
In the spring, the trees are full of small leaves.

Complex Sentences with *Until*
The cheetah ran until it caught the gazelle.

Writing Practice Write about someone who visits a biome (WB)

- **Writing**
  Write a fictional story (WB)
- **Project**
  Act in a play
- **Review**
  Units 17 and 18 (WB)
  Big Question 9 Review

Life in a Different Biome
Children discuss biomes where they would like to live

Listening Strategy
Listening for reasons

Asking About Needs
What do I need for my trip?

Complex Sentences with *Since* and *Because*
Since coral reefs are dying, we have to help them.

Writing Practice Write about protecting biomes (WB)

WRITE
a compare and
contrast report.

CREATE
a model of the
solar system.

BIG QUESTION ①

Where are we in the universe?

A Watch the video.

B Look at the picture and talk about it.

1 What is the girl looking at? What does it do?

2 What do you think the girl is thinking about?

C Think and answer the questions.

1 What can you see in the night sky where you live?

2 Where would you go if you were an astronaut? Why?

D Fill out the **Big Question Chart**.

What do you know about the universe? What do you want to know?

Words

A Listen and read the words. Listen again and say the words. 🔊 1·02

moon

asteroid

comet

meteorite

solar system

stars

galaxy

universe

spacecraft

telescope

observatory

B Write the following words in the correct order. Talk about your answers.

| solar system | meteorite | galaxy | moon | ~~universe~~ |

Largest ⟶ **Smallest**

_____universe_____ _____ _____ _____ _____

C Two of the three words are correct. Cross out the wrong answer.

1 People built this.
   observatory   ~~star~~   spacecraft

2 This is bright in the night sky.
   star   comet   meteorite

3 People use this to look at places far away.
   moon   observatory   telescope

4 This travels through space.
   asteroid   telescope   comet

Before You Read

Think Talk about the word *home* with your partner. What do you think of when you hear this word?

D **Learn** Visualizing Changes

Remember, you can make pictures in your mind by **visualizing** what you read. Think about how these pictures change as you read. This will help you to understand and remember a story or a poem.

Read. How do the pictures change in your mind? Write.

> Jon's spacecraft flew quickly through space. Through the window, the moon was small and bright. On the next day, it looked like a huge white ball with a bumpy surface and large, dark spots. On the third day, Jon's spacecraft circled the moon. The gray surface was just below him. Rocks of many different sizes covered the surface.

1 First: <u>I see the moon far away in the distance. It looks small and bright.</u>

2 Next: _____

_____

3 Finally: _____

_____

E **Words in Context** Scan the story on pages 10–11 and circle these words. As you read, guess what the words mean.

> **vast   dwelled   speck   disk**

F Answer the questions before you read.

1 Where are you right now? What is this place like?
2 What would this place look like if you went a kilometer into the sky?
3 What would it look like at 10 and 100 kilometers into the sky?

PREVIEW

Bella's Home

In this *science fiction* story, a science teacher in Nome, Alaska, writes a poem to help his daughter understand how vast and beautiful the universe is. As you read, try to visualize the changes that she sees on her journey through the universe.

Nome

Bella's Home

Charles Kunayak was a high school science teacher who lived with his family in a quiet neighborhood in Nome, Alaska. In his free time, he studied the secrets of the universe. Charles had a powerful telescope, and he often visited observatories, so he learned more and more about the universe. What an amazing universe!

Yet how could Charles help his daughter Bella understand that our sun was just one of billions* of stars? How could she realize that the small meteorite on display in his classroom traveled to Earth from beyond Mars? How could he explain that we live in a universe so vast, it would take a spacecraft 100,000 years to cross our Milky Way galaxy while traveling at the speed of light!

Charles decided that the best way to show Bella was not through numbers and charts, but through a poem. He sat down and wrote what he knew about the universe. He called it "Bella's Home."

Bella's Home

Bella lived in a white wooden house
On a street in the city of Nome.
Bella sat in her bedroom and thought to herself,
Where in the world is my home?

What I need, she thought, is a spacecraft
To give me a better view.
So in her mind, she climbed inside
And up in the sky she flew.

Her white wooden house was tiny indeed,
And Nome was as small as a pie.
As Bella flew up, she saw that Alaska
Looked like a bear from the sky.

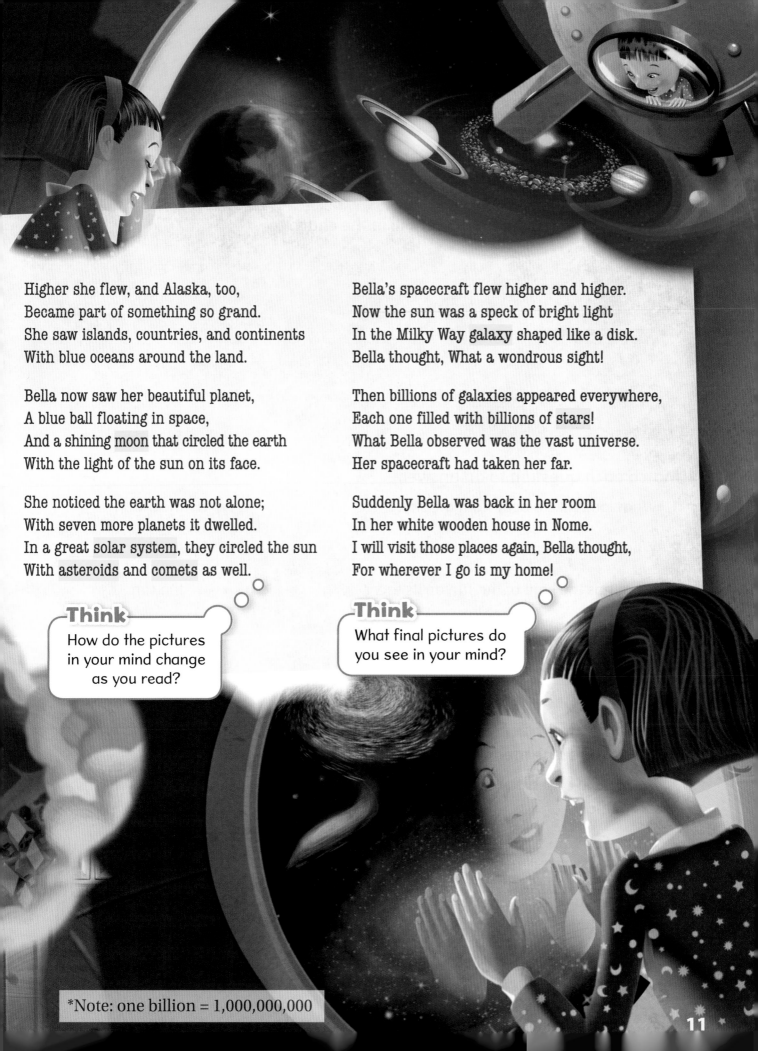

Higher she flew, and Alaska, too,
Became part of something so grand.
She saw islands, countries, and continents
With blue oceans around the land.

Bella now saw her beautiful planet,
A blue ball floating in space,
And a shining moon that circled the earth
With the light of the sun on its face.

She noticed the earth was not alone;
With seven more planets it dwelled.
In a great solar system, they circled the sun
With asteroids and comets as well.

Bella's spacecraft flew higher and higher.
Now the sun was a speck of bright light
In the Milky Way galaxy shaped like a disk.
Bella thought, What a wondrous sight!

Then billions of galaxies appeared everywhere,
Each one filled with billions of stars!
What Bella observed was the vast universe.
Her spacecraft had taken her far.

Suddenly Bella was back in her room
In her white wooden house in Nome.
I will visit those places again, Bella thought,
For wherever I go is my home!

Think

How do the pictures
in your mind change
as you read?

Think

What final pictures do
you see in your mind?

*Note: one billion = 1,000,000,000

Understand

Comprehension

 Think Do you understand the universe better after reading the poem about Bella's travels? Why or why not?

A In the poem, what did Bella see? Fill in the chart.

First	Next	Finally

B Match each question to an answer.

1 What looks like a bear from the sky? •   • **a** the moon

2 What is a blue ball floating in space? •   • **b** Alaska

3 What has the light of the sun on its face? •   • **c** the sun

4 What is a speck of bright light in the Milky Way? •   • **d** the universe

5 What has billions of galaxies? •   • **e** Earth

C **Words in Context** Read each line of poetry. Circle the word that has the same meaning as the underlined word.

1 What Bella observed was the <u>vast</u> universe.
    cold   huge   silent

2 With seven more planets it <u>dwelled</u>.
    lived   sang   fell

3 Now the sun was a <u>speck</u> of bright light.
    large ball   warm fire   small spot

4 The Milky Way galaxy was shaped like a <u>disk</u>.
    star   triangle   round plate

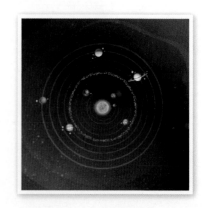

Grammar in Use

D Listen and read along. 🔊 1·04

Harry, what do you want to do in your life?

I want to travel through the universe.

Harry, do you want to sleep under the stars tonight?

No. I will miss my bed too much.

E Read the sentences. Which one is about what Harry believes?

a I will miss my bed too much.   **b** I want to travel through the universe.

F **Learn Grammar** Predictions with *Will*

Use **will** to make a prediction. A prediction is something you believe about the future. A prediction is not a fact.

I will visit those places again, Bella thought.

Three of the following sentences are predictions. Write P beside them. Write X beside the sentence that is not a prediction.

1 Scientists will send a person to Mars someday. _____

2 The sun will rise tomorrow morning. _____

3 She will become an astronaut when she grows up. _____

4 Eric will go to space camp next summer. _____

I think scientists will find new solar systems in our galaxy.

G Make a list like this one. Make predictions and then talk to your partner about them.

Things I Predict
Scientists will find new solar systems.

Communicate

Listening

 Think Why do people like to look up at the stars at night?

A **Learn** Listening for Reasons

When you listen for reasons, first listen for questions starting with the word *why*. The answer to each question will usually have a reason.

Listen. Match each question with a reason. 1·05

1 Why are stars so easy to see on Grandpa's farm? •

• **a** It's close to Earth and has clouds that bounce sunlight to Earth.

2 Why is Venus so bright? •

• **b** It's shaped like a disk. We are in the disk, and we can look through it.

3 Why can we see the Milky Way galaxy when we're in it? •

• **c** There are fewer lights shining outside of a big city.

B **Listen again. Why is our galaxy called the Milky Way? Write your answer.** 1·06

_____

_____

Speaking 1·07

C **Look at the two pictures. Talk about the differences with your partner.**

In the first picture, I see the Milky Way.

In the second picture, I see ...

The first picture has ...

The second picture doesn't have ... , but ...

Word Study

D **Learn** Words with *ei*

The vowel combination **ei** often has a *long a* sound.

Charles lived in a quiet neighborhood in Nome, Alaska.

Listen and read the words. Look them up in the dictionary. Then listen to the sentences. Write the *ei* words you hear in your notebook. 🔊 1·08

> **eighty   freight   reins   sleigh   veil   weigh**

 page 186

Writing Study

E **Learn** Complete Sentences

Complete sentences always need a subject and a verb. This is true for statements, questions, and commands. We usually don't see the subject in a command, but we understand what it is.

Earth revolves around the sun. (statement)
Is the sun in the Milky Way galaxy? (question)
Sit down. (command meaning *You sit down.*)

Read the paragraph. Circle two commands. Underline three incomplete sentences and rewrite them as complete sentences in your notebook.

> The universe is a beautiful place. <u>A mysterious place</u>. It has more stars than we can count. Old stars and new stars. (Try to count them) Our galaxy is the Milky Way. Look in the sky. Can you see a belt? A milky, white belt? That's our galaxy!

 Write Now practice writing in the **Workbook** page 9

BIG QUESTION ❶

Where are we in the universe?

We're on a planet in a solar system.

We're in a galaxy called the Milky Way.

Words

A Listen and say the words. Then read and listen to the sentences. 🔊 1·09

| astronomer | space probe | core | gravity | orbit | matter |

| distance | diameter | surface | craters | unique |

1 The **astronomer** studied the moons of Jupiter.

2 Scientists sent a **space probe** to Mars.

3 The **core** of Earth is 1,800 miles below the surface.

4 Without **gravity**, people on Earth would float into the air.

5 Earth's **orbit** around the sun is not a perfect circle.

6 Planets and stars are full of **matter**.

7 There is a big **distance** between the sun and Earth.

8 The **diameter** of Venus is similar to the diameter of Earth.

9 Many plants and animals live on our planet's **surface**.

10 You can see the moon's **craters** with a telescope.

11 Earth is **unique** because it has living creatures.

B Two of the three words are correct. Cross out the wrong answer.

1 Some people study this.

   matter   unique   gravity

2 You use this to measure something.

   distance   diameter   craters

3 This is part of Earth.

   orbit   surface   core

4 You can find this outside of Earth.

   space probe   astronomer   craters

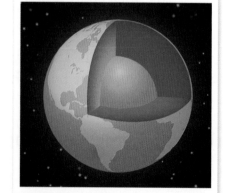

C How is Earth unique? Write a sentence. Then share your sentence with your partner.

Before You Read

Think Why is the sun important? How would life be different if we didn't have the sun?

D **Learn** Compare and Contrast in Science

Remember, when you **compare and contrast**, you talk about how things are alike and different. When you read about science, look for numbers and other information to decide how things are alike or different.

How are Proxima Centauri and the sun alike and different? Read the information and complete the diagram.

Proxima Centauri is the closest star to the sun. Did you know that the sun is also a star? They are both in the Milky Way galaxy. The sun is a yellow dwarf star. Proxima Centauri is a red dwarf star. Proxima Centauri's diameter is only $\frac{1}{7}$ of the sun's diameter.

Proxima Centauri   **The sun**

Different   Alike   Different

_____   _____   _____

_____   _____   _____

_____   _____   _____

_____   _____

E **Words in Context** Scan the reading on pages 18–19 and circle these words. As you read, guess what the words mean.

> bodies   explore   inner   outer

F Look at the pictures in the article on the next page. What do you see? What would you like to learn in this article?

PREVIEW

Traveling Together Around the Sun

In this *science article*, you will learn about the planets, moons, and other objects that move around the sun as a solar system. Science articles are full of facts and information about our world and universe. As you read, compare and contrast objects in our solar system.

Science: Astronomy

Traveling Together Around the Sun

The Asteroid Belt

An asteroid belt runs between the inner and outer planets. Scientists have discovered over 7,000 asteroids there, and there may be millions more. Asteroids travel around the sun, just like planets.

The sun is a star, and it is very important for our planet Earth. It gives us light and heat. However, Earth is not alone. It shares the sun with seven other planets. Together, these planets revolve around the sun in a solar system. Other bodies travel in this solar system, such as moons, asteroids, and comets. They all move around the sun because the sun's gravity is very strong.

Each planet's path around the sun is called an orbit. The planets that are closer to the sun have smaller orbits, so they take less time to go around it. Mercury takes 88 days to complete one orbit. Earth completes one orbit in 365 days, or one year. Neptune's orbit takes 60,200 days, or almost 165 years!

Each planet in our solar system is unique. For example, Mercury is the smallest planet. It has lots of craters, just like our moon. Jupiter is the biggest planet. Its diameter is eleven times bigger than Earth's. Saturn has giant rings of matter around it. Neptune is the farthest planet from the sun.

Mars is a neighboring planet, and scientists are learning a lot about it. They send many space probes to Mars. A space probe called Curiosity landed on Mars on August 6, 2012. Curiosity is as big as a car, and it moves over the surface of Mars. It recently found rocks that had strange shapes. Running water made these shapes. This is an important discovery. Space probes like Curiosity continue to explore the planets, moons, and other bodies in our solar system. If technology continues to grow, we will travel to these places ourselves.

Iron and rock make up most of the four smaller inner planets of our solar system. Gas and water make up most of the four larger outer planets. This means that you can stand on the surface of Earth, but you can't stand on Saturn. In fact, if you tried to stand on Saturn, you would sink down to the core of the planet.

Drawings of our solar system show the planets close to the sun. However, the distance between the planets and the sun is very far. For example, it would take 176 years to drive a car from Earth to the sun. It would take 5,300 years to drive from Neptune to the sun!

Astronomers think that there are many solar systems in our Milky Way galaxy. However, our solar system is special to us. It is our home.

Think

How are the inner planets the same? How are they different from the outer planets?

Think

How are some of the planets different from Earth?

The Sister Planets

Did you know that Earth and Venus are called "sister planets"? This is because they are almost the same size, and Venus is the closest planet to Earth. However, Venus is much hotter than Earth, and it is always covered in thick clouds.

Comprehension

 Think What interesting facts did you learn about our solar system? Discuss your ideas with your partner.

A How are the planets below alike and different? Complete the diagram.

Earth **Venus**

Different   Alike   Different

_____   _____   _____

_____   _____   _____

_____   _____   _____

_____   _____

B Circle True (T) or False (F).

1 Mercury and our moon both have craters.   T   F

2 Mars once had flowing water.   T   F

3 You can stand on the surfaces of the outer planets.   T   F

4 There are only a few asteroids in our solar system.   T   F

C **Words in Context** Match the sentence parts.

1 Space probes explore planets and moons. **Explore** means …   • • **a** … far from the center.

2 Many bodies travel in space. **Bodies** means …   • • **b** … close to the center.

3 Mercury, Venus, Earth, and Mars are inner planets. **Inner** means …   • • **c** … to travel around a new place to learn about it.

4 Jupiter, Saturn, Uranus, and Neptune are outer planets. **Outer** means …   • • **d** … large objects in space.

Grammar in Use

D Listen and sing along. **Going into Space** 🔊 1·11

If I become an astronaut,
I'll fly up through the stars.
I'll travel in a spacecraft,
And I will go to Mars!
I'll explore the planet's surface,
Its craters and dry lakes.
Life will be so interesting
If I go into space!

E Read the sentence. What has to happen before the speaker will go to Mars?

If I become an astronaut, I will go to Mars.

F **Learn Grammar** Future Real Conditional

Use the **future real conditional** to talk about a future possibility and what will happen as a result of it. Use the word **if** with a future possibility.

If technology continues to grow, we will travel to these places ourselves.
└─────── future possibility ───────┘ └─────────── result ───────────┘

We will travel to these places ourselves if technology continues to grow.
└─────────── result ───────────┘ └─────── future possibility ───────┘

Read each sentence. Draw a line under the future possibility. Draw two lines under the result.

1 If I become an astronaut, I will walk on the surface of Mars.

2 Wendy will search the sky if she gets a telescope.

3 If we study hard, the teacher will show us a video.

> If I study hard, I will get good grades.

G Make a chart like this one. Then talk to your partner about it.

This will happen in the future ...	... if this happens first.
I will get good grades.	I study hard.

Communicate

Listening

 Think If you could travel at the speed of light, which planet in our solar system would you visit? Why?

A Listen. What is the main idea? Write. 🔊 1·12

_____

B Listen again. Write the travel times at the speed of light. 🔊 1·13

Traveling in Space at the Speed of Light		
From	**To**	**Travel Time**
The sun	Earth	**8 minutes**
Earth	Mars	
Earth	Jupiter	
Earth	Neptune	
Earth	The nearest star	

Speaking 🔊 1·14

C **Learn** Asking About Quantity

Use **how much** to ask about things you cannot count. Use **how many** to ask about things you can count.

How much water is on Jupiter?
How many planets are in our solar system?

Ask and answer questions about quantity with your partner.

How many stars does our solar system have?

It has ...

How much ... ?

I'm not sure, but ...

Word Study

 Learn Words with the Suffixes *-ance* and *-ant*

Many nouns that end in **-ance** can become adjectives if you change the ending to **-ant**.

Neptune is a long distance **from the sun.** (noun)

Neptune is a distant **planet from the sun.** (adjective)

Listen and read the words. Look them up in the dictionary. Circle *-ance* **or** *-ant* **in each word. Then listen to the sentences. Write the** *-ance* **or** *-ant* **word you hear in the correct space.** 1•15

| fragrance | arrogance | ignorance | fragrant | arrogant | ignorant |

A-Z page 186

Noun

1 _____fragrance_____ 2 _____ 3 _____

Adjective

4 _____ 5 _____ 6 _____

Writing Study

 Learn Choice Questions

A question can offer a choice between two or more things. Use the word **or** in **choice questions**. The answer is never *yes* or *no*.

Is Ganymede a planet or **a moon?**   **It's a moon.**

Is Proxima Centauri bigger or **smaller than the sun?**   **It's smaller.**

Circle *or* **in each question. Underline the choices. Then write.**

1 Is Mars <u>a moon</u>, <u>a planet</u>, or <u>a star</u>? _____ It's a planet. _____

2 Does Earth go around the sun or around the moon? _____

3 Is Jupiter bigger or smaller than Earth? _____

 Now practice writing in the Workbook. page 17

Vocabulary: Words with the Suffixes -ance and -ant • Writing: Choice Questions **Unit 2** **23**

Wrap Up

Writing

A Read this compare and contrast report about an imaginary solar system.

Title — The FWCP Solar System

Introduction — What is it like to live in a solar system filled with color? In my imagination, I visited the FWCP solar system in the Milky Way galaxy. FWCP means "Filled with Colorful Planets." FWCP and our solar system are alike in many ways, but there are also many differences between them.

Similarities — FWCP and our solar system are alike in three important ways. First, FWCP has eight planets that travel around a star like our sun. Next, FWCP has an asteroid belt like ours. Finally, the inner planets of FWCP are smaller than the outer planets, just like in our solar system.

Differences — However, FWCP is different than our solar system. First, each planet in FWCP has a bright, colorful surface. Some planets in our solar system are not as colorful. Next, there are no moons in FWCP. Finally, all the inner planets in FWCP have people. In our solar system, only Earth has people.

Conclusion — FWCP is an interesting place. I will visit it again very soon. When I compare FWCP to our solar system, I can understand more about the universe.

B Answer the questions.

1 How are the two solar systems alike?
2 How are the two solar systems different?

Review the Writing Process
- Brainstorm your ideas and write them down.
- Organize your ideas into groups.
- Take your ideas and put them into paragraphs.
- Revise what you wrote.

Learn Compare and Contrast Report

- Start your report with an introduction paragraph.
- Describe how two things are alike in the second paragraph.
- Describe how two things are different in the third paragraph.
- End your report with a conclusion paragraph. This should have a strong, final thought.

 Write Now go to the **Workbook** to plan and write your own compare and contrast report. page 18

Project: Creating a Model

C Create a model of the solar system. Then present it.

- In your group, you will make a solar system model.

- Decide what you will use to make the model, who will make each part, which parts your group will compare and contrast, and what each student will say.

- Write down some words to help you remember your ideas.

- Use compare and contrast words, such as *but* and *however*.

- Practice your presentation with your group.

- Show your model and give your presentation to the class.

- Make eye contact with other students, gesture toward your model, and speak in a loud, clear voice.

Here is the sun. It is the star in our solar system.

This is Earth, where we live!

Planets orbit the sun.

BIG QUESTION ①

Where are we in the universe?

A Watch the video.

B Think more about the Big Question. What did you learn?

C Complete the **Big Question Chart**.

What did you learn about our place in the universe?

In units **3** and **4** you will:

WATCH
a video about uncovering the past.

LEARN
how we know about the past.

READ
about ancient soldiers and a boy's discovery.

WRITE
a descriptive report.

CREATE
a time capsule.

BIG QUESTION 2

How do we know what happened long ago?

A Watch the video. ▶

B Look at the picture and talk about it.

1 What is the boy taking a picture of? Why is he taking a picture?

2 Where do you think the boy is? What else do you think is in this place?

C Think and answer the questions.

1 Why do people want to learn about the past?

2 What time in the past do you want to learn more about?

D Fill out the **Big Question Chart**.

What do you know about studying the past? What do you want to know?

Words

A Listen and read the words. Listen again and say the words. 🔊 1·16

| army | soldiers | uniform | emperor | armor | treasure |

| archaeologist | tomb | jade | clay | peasant |

B Write the following words in the correct places on the chart below. Then talk about your answers.

> armor   clay   emperor   jade   soldiers
> archaeologist   peasant   uniforms

People	Things to Wear	Things to Create Something

C Circle the correct answer.

1 This is worth a lot of money.
   clay   treasure

2 Some people are buried in this.
   tomb   army

3 This keeps a country or town safe.
   army   peasant

4 This keeps a person's body safe.
   uniform   armor

Before You Read

 Think When someone discovers an important item from the past, who should it belong to? Why?

D **Learn** Author's Purpose

Every author has a **purpose**, or reason, for writing. There are three main purposes.

Persuade: to make you believe or do something
Inform: to give you information or facts
Entertain: to make you enjoy the story

Circle the author's purpose for each paragraph. Talk about your answers with a partner.

1

> The copper coin's diameter is 23 millimeters. It has the name and face of a Roman emperor on it. He ruled from AD 306 to 337.

     to persuade   to inform   to entertain

2

> The archaeologist looked into the dark tomb. He was excited, but he was nervous, too. Slowly, he stepped forward. His torch brightened a room full of gold and jewels!

     to persuade   to inform   to entertain

3

> We should not sell old treasure that we find. We should display it in museums. The history of the world belongs to its people.

     to persuade   to inform   to entertain

E **Words in Context** Scan the reading on pages 30–31 and circle these words. As you read, guess what the words mean.

| battle | generals | varnish | coffin |

F Look at the pictures of the clay soldiers in the reading. How would you describe them to someone who doesn't know what they look like?

Hidden Army:
Clay Soldiers of Ancient China

In this *magazine article*, you will read about the discovery of a large army of clay soldiers in China. A magazine article gives information and often has colorful pictures. As you read, remember to ask yourself about the author's purpose.

Social Studies: History

Jane O'Connor is the bestselling author of over 30 books for children, including the fun and popular *Fancy Nancy* series. She lives in New York City.

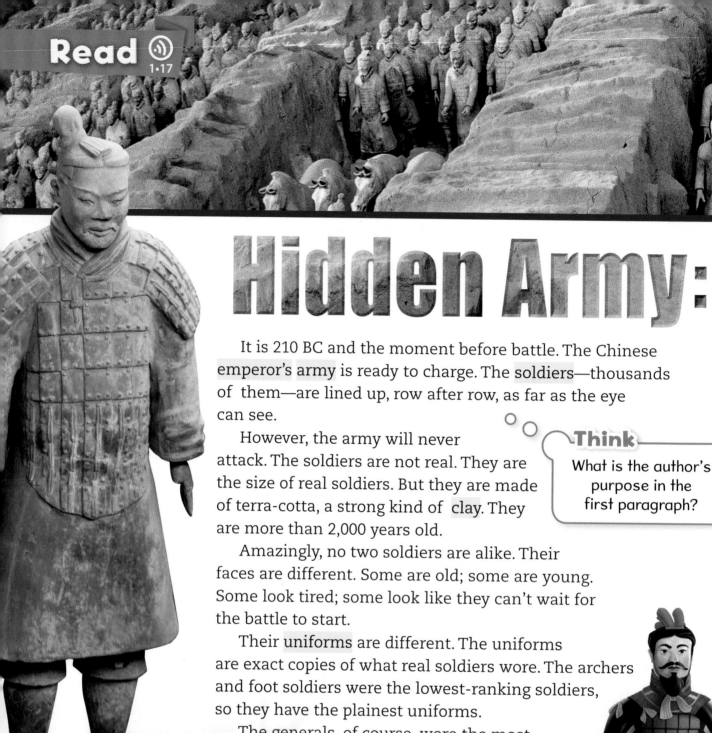

Hidden Army:

It is 210 BC and the moment before battle. The Chinese emperor's army is ready to charge. The soldiers—thousands of them—are lined up, row after row, as far as the eye can see.

However, the army will never attack. The soldiers are not real. They are the size of real soldiers. But they are made of terra-cotta, a strong kind of clay. They are more than 2,000 years old.

Think

What is the author's purpose in the first paragraph?

Amazingly, no two soldiers are alike. Their faces are different. Some are old; some are young. Some look tired; some look like they can't wait for the battle to start.

Their uniforms are different. The uniforms are exact copies of what real soldiers wore. The archers and foot soldiers were the lowest-ranking soldiers, so they have the plainest uniforms.

The generals, of course, wore the most elegant uniforms. Some of their caps had feathers. Sometimes their shoes turned up at the toes. Their armor had small iron rings that look like fish scales.

Think

What is the author's purpose for this paragraph?

Here you see an image of a clay general. It shows how he looked 2,000 years ago. Every single soldier in the emperor's army was painted with bright colors. So were the terra-cotta horses. Now most of the soldiers have only tiny traces of paint left. Scientists are trying to create a special varnish to brush over painted figures to hold the paint in place.

a computerized image of a clay general

Clay Soldiers of Ancient China

Today, craftsmen near the pits where the soldiers were found make copies of the soldiers. This helps archaeologists learn more about how people made the original army. Modern craftsmen have much better kilns than those in ancient times. Kilns are ovens that bake clay until it hardens. Yet no copies ever come out as hard or shiny as the originals. Why? Nobody knows—it is a mystery.

An even bigger mystery is what lies inside the emperor's tomb. Nobody knows the answer because the tomb has never been opened. The Chinese government plans to keep it closed for now. Work will not start until archaeologists are sure the tomb can be opened without damaging any of the treasures inside.

As for the emperor's body, according to historical records, it rests in a heavy, bronze coffin.

In ancient times, the custom was to dress the dead body of someone important in a suit the Chinese made from hundreds of pieces of thin jade. At that time, jade was more precious than gold.

The emperor died when he was 49 years old. Three years after his death, peasants rose up against the empire. One of their leaders started a new royal family.

Yet now, millions of people come to the emperor's burial place. They visit the covered pits to see the clay soldiers. The emperor lives on in the memory of all who see his amazing hidden army.

Think

What is the author's purpose for the entire reading?

Understand

Comprehension

 Think What does the discovery of the terra-cotta soldiers teach you? What else do you want to know about life in China 2,000 years ago?

A What is the author's purpose for each sentence below? Write the number for each sentence in the correct box. Talk about your answers with your partner.

1 The Chinese emperor's army is ready to charge.
2 The emperor died when he was 49 years old.
3 The terra-cotta soldiers are more than 2,000 years old.
4 It is the moment before battle.
5 Some look like they can't wait for the battle to start.
6 Their armor had small iron rings that look like fish scales.

To Inform	To Entertain
	1

B Circle True (T) or False (F).

1 Every terra-cotta soldier looks exactly the same.   T   F

2 The terra-cotta horses were colorful a long time ago.   T   F

3 The original clay soldiers were shinier than the copies.   T   F

4 Archaeologists know what's inside the emperor's tomb.   T   F

5 Many people come to see the terra-cotta soldiers.   T   F

C **Words in Context** Match each word to its definition. Write the letter.

1 battle _____   **a** a clear liquid that keeps something looking new

2 general _____   **b** a box that a dead body is put into

3 varnish _____   **c** a fight between armies in a war

4 coffin _____   **d** a very important officer in an army

Grammar in Use

D Listen and sing along. **The Archaeologist** 🔊 1·18

I'm an archaeologist,
And I love to study the past.
I like to hunt and then to dig
And uncover things at last!

A piece of ancient armor,
Or jade or cloth or clay,
I promise to share my treasures
To show the past today.

E Look at **D**. Which verbs start with *to*?

F **Learn Grammar** Verbs Followed by Infinitives

Some verbs are often followed by an **infinitive**. An infinitive is a verb with the word **to** in front of it.

The Chinese government plans to keep it closed for now.
verb   infinitive

Match the two parts of each sentence. Then circle the infinitives.

1 All the students promised •

2 The archeologists tried •

3 The emperor decided •

• **a** to find more terra-cotta soldiers.

• **b** to build the clay army.

• **c** to study hard for the history test.

G Make a chart like this one. Use infinitives with the verbs *forgot* and *promise*. Then talk about your ideas with a partner.

I forgot to pack my lunch today.

I forgot ...	I promise ...
to pack my lunch	

Communicate

Listening

 Think How were people's lives in the past different from your life?

A **Learn** Listening for Similarities and Differences

When you listen to people talking about the past, try to listen for similarities and differences with the present time.

Listen and match. 🔊 1·19

Ancient Town

1 The houses had an upstairs floor and a downstairs floor. •

2 It had a stone wall around it. •

3 Salt was valuable and kept food fresh. •

Now

• **a** This product is now cheap. Refrigerators keep food fresh.

• **b** Many modern houses have this, too.

• **c** Modern towns don't have this around them.

B **Listen again. Write the correct answer.** 🔊 1·20

1 Where did the students get their information? _____

2 How old is the ancient town? _____

3 How were bricks made in this town? _____

Speaking 🔊 1·21

C If you had a time machine, what place and time would you like to go back to and visit? Talk about it with your partner and give reasons.

I'd like to go back to ancient Greece.

Why would you choose that place?

I'd like to see ... What about you?

I'd like to ...

Word Study

D Learn — Words with the Suffix -ist

The suffix **-ist** is often used for jobs or professions.

This helps an archaeologist learn more about how people made the original army.

Listen and read the words. Circle the suffixes. Then listen to the sentences. Write the *-ist* words you hear in your notebook. 1·22

> cyclist   cartoonist   dentist   florist   tourist   pianist
>
> **A-Z**

Writing Study

E Learn — Verb Tenses

Keep your **verb tenses** the same in a paragraph or a piece of writing. This will help your writing be clear.

The first emperor died when he was 49 years old. Three years after his death, peasants rose up against the empire.

Read the paragraph. Cross out and change the verbs that are in the wrong tense.

In 2007, a man in Vienna had a garden. He ~~uncovers~~ **uncovered** over 200 pieces of buried treasure. He finds rings, belt buckles, and many other items that were over 650 years old. Later, he took the treasure to a government office. The people there are very excited when they see the rare items. They wait in a long line to see the treasure that the man find.

 Write Now practice writing in the **Workbook.** page 28

BIG QUESTION 2

How do we know what happened long ago?

We uncover and study old objects.

Archaeologists help us understand the objects.

Words

A Listen and read the words. Listen again and say the words. 🔊 1·23

dinosaur

skull

ravine

examine

discover

excavate

layers

paleontologist

ash

sedimentary rock

pastime

B Circle True (T) or False (F).

1 Dinosaurs are alive on Earth today.   T   F

2 Burning wood can make ash.   T   F

3 Sedimentary rock is in the ground.   T   F

4 A layer is round like a ball.   T   F

5 Plants have skulls.   T   F

6 Studying at school is a pastime.   T   F

7 A ravine can be hard to climb out of.   T   F

C Answer the questions.

1 What do paleontologists examine? _____

_____

2 Why do people excavate an area when they discover a bone there?

_____

_____

Before You Read

 Think Why do people like to find objects from the past?
What can you learn from an old object?

D Learn Predictions

A **prediction** is what you think will happen. As you read, try to make predictions. Use clues from the reading and your own knowledge to predict. You can predict by using the word *will*.

What the Story Says	My Prediction
Dark clouds cover the sky.	Rain will come.

Read the sentences below. Predict what will happen. Write.

1

Jamaal hiked for four hours in the hot sun this afternoon. Then he came home and ate a big dinner. Finally, he worked on his homework for two hours. Now he is very tired.

I predict _____

2

The paleontologist uncovered many of the dinosaur's bones in the ravine. However, she didn't have the skull yet. Suddenly, she brushed the dirt away from a large, shiny bone in the ground. A huge smile spread over her face.

I predict _____

E Words in Context Scan the story on pages 38–39 and circle these words. As you read, guess what the words mean.

> favorite   dream   tripped   determine

F Answer the questions before you read.

1 What do curious people do when they find something new?
2 When were you curious about something? What were you curious about?
3 Is it good to be curious? Why or why not?

PREVIEW

Stumbling upon the Past

In this *realistic fiction* story, a boy named Javier makes an amazing discovery in his small town in Spain. A realistic fiction story has characters, problems, and settings that seem real. As you read, try to predict what will happen throughout the story.

Ademuz

Stumbling upon the Past

Javier was a nine-year-old boy who lived with his parents in the hillside town of Ademuz in the province of Valencia in Spain. Javier was a curious and energetic boy. His favorite pastime was to explore the hills and open fields around his town.

The neighboring village of Riodeva, just 26 kilometers away from Ademuz, was famous because of a great discovery there. In 2003, paleontologists found the bones of the largest dinosaur in Europe in a wheat field near the little village. When it was alive, this animal was over 38 meters long and had the weight of seven elephants.

Javier liked dinosaurs more than anything else in the world. He also believed that there was an amazing dinosaur bone buried somewhere near his own town of Ademuz. His dream was to be the first person to find it.

One summer morning, Javier was exploring in a field near a ravine just outside of the town. He looked up to see his two friends, Fernando and Pepe, running toward him with a colorful kite.

Think

Do you think that Javier will be the first person to find a bone? Why or why not?

"Let's fly it, Javier!" they shouted.

Javier enjoyed playing with his friends. He quickly forgot about his exploring and grabbed the string of the kite. As he ran, the kite lifted into the sky. The boys cheered. Suddenly the kite spun around and dove into the ravine.

"I'll get it," shouted Javier. He ran down into the ravine. As he reached for the kite, his foot caught on something. He fell to the rocky ground with a crash. His two friends ran up as he rubbed his head.

"Are you okay?" Pepe asked.

"I think so," said Javier. He looked down at a rough, gray object sticking out of the ground. "I tripped on that," he said.

"It looks like a rock," said Fernando.

Javier looked carefully at the object. "I don't think it's a rock," he said excitedly. "I think it's something else!"

"Let's pull it out," said Pepe.

"No," said Javier. "It's better to leave it right here."

Javier and the boys ran home to tell Javier's parents. Javier's father spoke to the mayor of the town, who contacted the Paleontology Foundation. The next day, a paleontologist from the foundation came to the town. He followed Javier to the ravine and examined the boy's discovery.

"It could be a dinosaur bone," he said. "If it is, we'll need to determine how old it is."

"How do you do that?" asked Javier.

"This bone was buried in sedimentary rock, which lies in layers under the ground. We'll look for volcanic ash below and above this rock layer. Through a special process, we can find out the ages of those layers of ash. Then we'll know that the dinosaur died sometime between those two ages."

Soon, many paleontologists began excavating the area around the bone. They found more bones, as well as a skull. It was a unique dinosaur they didn't know about. Television reporters came to the town and spoke to Javier about the bone he discovered.

"This dinosaur will need a name," said one reporter. "What do you think it should be called?"

"That's easy," said the man from the Paleontology Foundation. "We'll call it the Javiersaurus!"

Think

Predict what the rough, gray object is.

Think

What do you predict the dinosaur will be called?

39

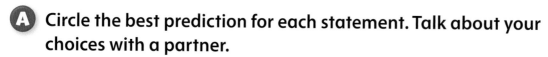

Understand

Comprehension

Think Talk about the story with your partner. Do you think it could really happen? Why or why not?

A Circle the best prediction for each statement. Talk about your choices with a partner.

1 The paleontologists found all the bones of Javier's dinosaur. What will happen next?

   a They will stop looking and go back to their homes.

   b They will ask Javier to look for more bones.

   c They will look for more dinosaur bones in the ravine.

2 The dinosaur will be called the Javiersaurus. What will happen next?

   a Fernando and Pepe will be angry.

   b Fernando and Pepe will be happy for Javier.

   c Fernando and Pepe will not be friends with Javier.

3 Javier is very interested in dinosaurs. What will happen next?

   a He will become a paleontologist someday.

   b He will become a mayor someday.

   c He will stop looking for dinosaur bones.

B Answer the questions.

1 How was the dinosaur in Riodeva special?

2 Why was Javier in the field when Fernando and Pepe ran up to him?

3 What do paleontologists look for above and below sedimentary rock?

C **Words in Context** Match each sentence to an explanation.

1 His <u>favorite</u> pastime was to explore the open fields.   •

  • **a** This means that he always thought about doing this thing someday.

2 His <u>dream</u> was to be the first person to find it.   •

  • **b** This means that they need to find out or discover this information.

3 "We'll need to <u>determine</u> how old it is."   •

  • **c** This means that he hit his foot against something and fell down.

4 "I <u>tripped</u> on that," he said.   •

  • **d** This means that he enjoyed doing this activity more than any other activity.

Grammar in Use

D Listen and read along. 🔊 1·25

E Read the sentences below. Which words end in *-ing*?

a I don't like getting my hands dirty.　　**b** Now they enjoy digging in the garden!

F **Learn Grammar**　Verbs Followed by Gerunds

Remember, **gerunds** are verbs that end in *-ing*. Gerunds can act like nouns.
Verbs like *enjoy*, *finish*, and *practice* are often followed by gerunds.

Javier enjoyed playing with his friends.
verb　　gerund

Read each sentence. Circle the gerunds. Underline the verb in front of each gerund.

1 When it began raining, the excavation team went inside.

2 The museum staff finished cleaning the dinosaur bones.

3 Thomas liked examining fossils as a pastime.

4 The paleontologist doesn't like working in the rain.

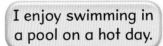

I enjoy swimming in a pool on a hot day.

G Make a chart like this one. Use gerunds.
Then talk about it with a partner.

I enjoy …	I don't like …
swimming	

Communicate

Listening

 What kinds of stories do your grandparents, parents, or teachers tell you?

A Listen. Why did the sun and the moon go into the sky? 🔊 1·26

_____

_____

B Listen again. Number the events in the correct order. 🔊 1·27

____ The ocean filled half of the house with water.

____ The ocean came to visit the sun's house.

__1__ The sun built a bigger house for the ocean.

____ The sun and the moon went up into the sky.

____ The ocean filled all of the house with water.

Speaking 🔊 1·28

C **Learn** Describing with the Senses

Use your senses to ask about and describe things.

What did dinosaurs sound like?
They probably sounded very loud.

You can also use other sense verbs, such as _look_, _taste_, and _feel_.

Ask your partner to describe something using one of the senses. Then describe something for your partner.

> What does a dinosaur bone feel like?

> It probably feels ... What do you think ... ?

> I think ...

> I agree. / No, I think it ...

Word Study

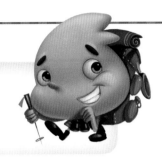

D **Learn** Words with *ie*

Together, the vowels **ie** can have a *long e* sound in a word.

Javier explored the open fields around his town.

Listen and read the words. Circle the vowels that make a *long e* sound. Then listen to the sentences. Write each *ie* word in your notebook. 🔊 1·29

thief   grief   relief   piece   brief   niece

A-Z

Writing Study

E **Learn** Count and Noncount Nouns

Count nouns can be singular (one thing) or plural (more than one thing). A singular count noun takes a singular verb. A plural count noun takes a plural verb.

The dinosaur <u>bone</u> is very large.
Many dinosaur <u>bones</u> are still buried under the ground.

Noncount nouns always take a singular verb.

A lot of volcanic <u>ash</u> was above the bone.
A little <u>water</u> is in the ravine.

Read the sentences. Circle the correct verb.

1 Sedimentary rock **was / were** above and below the bone.

2 Dinosaurs **was / were** on Earth a long time ago.

3 Light clothing **feel / feels** good when you are excavating in hot weather.

4 The skull **look / looks** like it might belong to a meat-eating dinosaur.

 Now practice writing in the Workbook. page 36 ▷

Wrap Up

Writing

A Read this descriptive report about an old photograph.

Title —— **A Picture from the Past**

Introduction —— Yesterday I found a picture of my great-grandfather when he was only ten years old. Because of this photograph, I learned a lot about the past.

Body —— In the picture, my great-grandfather stood on a farm with a basket of eggs. Far behind him was a chicken coop. I can imagine the clucking sounds of all the chickens. There was an old wooden bridge near the chicken coop. It was built over the river where my great-grandfather and his family washed their clothes.

My great-grandfather wore a simple cotton shirt, rough jeans, black leather shoes, and a wide straw hat to protect him from the sun. My mother said that people made some of their own clothes back then.

Conclusion —— Because of this picture, I learned that my great-grandfather lived simply. He worked hard on the farm to help his family. His family didn't have a lot of money, but my great-grandfather looked very happy and healthy.

B Answer the questions.

1 How did the great-grandfather and his family get food?
2 Why was the river important to the great-grandfather and his family?
3 Who do you think made the great-grandfather's clothes?

Learn Descriptive Report

- In the introduction, tell the reader about the subject you will describe.
- Describe your subject with many details in the body. Describe with your senses to paint a picture in your reader's mind, and use details to explain what you learned.
- Summarize what you learned in the conclusion paragraph.

 Write Now go to the **Workbook** to plan and write your descriptive report. page 37

Project: Creating a Time Capsule

C Create a time capsule of important items. Then present it.

- In your group, think of things that are important to you today. You will create a time capsule for these things.

- Choose your time capsule container. You can use a box, a bag, a backpack, or anything you have.

- Put real objects, photos, or drawings that show important things into your group's time capsule.

- For each item you put into the time capsule, write a short statement about why it is important.

- Practice your presentation with your group. Each member of the group should show at least one object from the time capsule and talk about it.

- With your group, present your time capsule to the class.

Stories are important to me, so I added a book.

I put a smartphone into the time capsule because it connects us to people.

TIME CAPSULE

Our time capsule also has a drawing of a forest. I think that nature is one of the most important things in the world.

BIG QUESTION 2

How do we know what happened long ago?

A Watch the video.

B Think more about the Big Question. What did you learn?

C Complete the **Big Question Chart.**

What did you learn about studying the past?

In units **5** and **6** you will:

WATCH
a video about the world of food.

LEARN
where the food you eat comes from.

READ
about a special breakfast and how far food travels.

BIG QUESTION ③

Where does our food come from?

A Watch the video. ▶

B Look at the picture and talk about it.

1 Where is the boy? What is he doing? What does he have in the cart?

2 What do you think the boy is thinking about? What will he do next?

C Think and answer the questions.

1 What foods do farmers grow in your area?

2 What are your favorite foods?

D Fill out the **Big Question Chart.**

What do you know about where food comes from? What do you want to know?

Words

A Listen and read the words. Listen again and say the words. 🔊 1·30

sugar cane

wheat

cinnamon

butter

vanilla

ingredients

bark

plantation

steamship

spoil

leopard

B Match each clue to a word. Write the correct letter.

1 This is alive and can be dangerous. ____　　　　　**a** steamship

2 You can see and feel this on the outside of a tree. ____　　**b** plantation

3 This carries people and things on water. ____　　　　　**c** sugar cane

4 You need these to make a pie. ____　　　　　　　　**d** leopard

5 Most bread is made from this. ____　　　　　　　　**e** wheat

6 On this land, people grow plants to eat or use. ____　　　**f** spoil

7 Something sweet comes from this plant. ____　　　　　**g** ingredients

8 If food does this, don't eat it. ____　　　　　　　　**h** bark

C What foods have butter, vanilla, or cinnamon? Why do you think foods have these ingredients? Talk about your answers with your partner.

Before You Read

 Think What ingredients are in your favorite dish or meal? Can you make that dish or meal? Why or why not?

D **Learn** Conclusions

> Use information in a reading together with your own knowledge to make a decision about something. This decision is a **conclusion**.

Read each paragraph. Then circle the correct conclusion.

1

> Vanilla comes from a bean. It is used to make vanilla ice cream, vanilla pudding, and other tasty snacks. Many people like the taste of chocolate, but some people prefer the taste of vanilla.

a Vanilla comes from cows.
b People use vanilla to make food taste good.
c Vanilla is the same as chocolate.

2

> Wheat is an important plant. It grows in many places around the world, but it is originally from the Middle East. People use wheat to make many foods, such as bread, pasta, and cake. Many people eat wheat every day.

a Everyone eats wheat.
b Wheat grows in every country.
c Wheat is very popular.

E **Words in Context** Scan the story on pages 50–51 and circle these words. As you read, guess what the words mean.

> **gather   introduce   peel   coax**

F **Answer the questions before you read.**

1 Do you travel to other places? If so, where did you go? What did you see? What did you eat?
2 How is food different in other countries across the world?

The Breakfast Quest

In this *humorous fiction* story, a young boy travels the world in search of ingredients. Humorous fiction stories have characters and events that are funny. As you read, stop and ask, *What is my conclusion?*

Author Charlotte Spektor writes children's stories that take place all across the world. She loves food and traveling, and these topics often show up in her stories.

The Breakfast Quest

I'm making a special breakfast today: Granny's Famous Cinnamon Buns. "To make the best buns, you need the best ingredients," I tell my sister Sam. So we hop on my bike and ride across town to Farmer Ray's.

"You've come to the right place," says the farmer, pulling on his bushy beard. "My chickens lay wonderful eggs."

At the chicken coop, I gather two smooth, brown eggs and a nervous chicken.

"Cinnamon buns, you say?" Farmer Ray smiles slyly. "If it's butter you're after, you'll need to pack your bags. The best butter I know comes from Denmark."

We all hop on his tractor, catch a plane, and watch as we zoom over the Atlantic Ocean.

In Demark, we head to rolling green fields where we find an enormous, sleepy cow. I introduce myself, my sister Sam, Farmer Ray, and the chicken to the cow's owner, explaining that my grandmother's cinnamon buns are not to be missed.

Think

Draw a conclusion. Could this story really happen?

"Well, you've come to the right place," says Farmer Lena, spilling some milk from a pail. "My butter is the creamiest in the world. Cinnamon buns, you say?" She pauses. "If it's flour you need, the heartiest wheat I know comes from France."

We all ride the cow to the train to France, where we find an amber field of warm, dry grain and meet a French farmer who listens very closely to our plan.

"Well you've come to the right place," says Farmer Francois, twirling his mustache.

"My wheat makes the very best flour in the entire world!" I grab two armfuls.

"Cinnamon buns, you say? If it's vanilla you need, the finest vanilla in all the world comes from Madagascar. Come with me!"

We all hop in his hot air balloon and set off over Africa, looking down on a magnificent leopard roaming the plains.

In Madagascar, we march through the lush hills. There we meet Sabine, a vanilla grower, and I tell her the plan.

"Well, if you're making famous cinnamon buns, you've come to the right place," says Farmer Sabine, her eyes sparkling. "My vines produce the most fragrant vanilla beans in all the world!"

I scoop up a handful of the heavy, brown vanilla beans.

"Madagascar grows sugar cane and cinnamon, too," says Farmer Sabine. "Let me take you to my friend Patrick's plantation." Patrick listens to the plan.

"True, I have the sweetest sugar cane and the very best cinnamon in the world," he says. "Sugar cane I can give you, but..." He looks sad. "I'm afraid I can't help you with cinnamon. I'm all out! We harvested it yesterday."

"No cinnamon for the cinnamon buns!" we cry. "Now what?"

Something high atop a tree catches my eye: a small area of bark. I climb the tree and peel some off. "This will do," I say, grinning at the relieved crowd.

We coax the cow and the chicken onto a steamship and head home before the ingredients spoil, mixing up a batch of Granny's Famous Cinnamon Buns along the way.

"Well?" I ask as everyone chews and smiles.

"You were right!" say the farmers. "These are truly the very best cinnamon buns in all the world!"

Now, what should I make for lunch?

Think

Draw a conclusion. What will the boy do now?

Understand

Comprehension

 What makes this story funny? Tell your partner about three funny events in the story. Then tell your partner if you think these events could really happen or not.

A Match the food to where it comes from. Use information from the story. You have to draw conclusions to match some of the items.

Where Do They Come From?

1 eggs ●   ● **a** cows

2 butter ●   ● **b** bark

3 flour ●   ● **c** chickens

4 cinnamon ●   ● **d** beans

5 sugar ●   ● **e** wheat

6 vanilla ●   ● **f** sugar cane

B Answer the questions.

1 Why does the boy go to so many different places?

_____

2 How did everyone get from Denmark to France?

_____

3 Why did the boy climb a tree in Madagascar?

_____

C **Words in Context** Match each verb to a definition.

1 gather ●   ● **a** to meet someone and tell them your name

2 coax ●   ● **b** to come or bring together in a group

3 introduce ●   ● **c** to take the outside part off of something

4 peel ●   ● **d** to try to get someone to do something

Grammar in Use

D Listen and sing along. **Vanilla Pudding** 🔊 1·32

We're making vanilla pudding tomorrow
With milk from a country cow
And sugar from Puerto Rico.
I'm dreaming about it now!
We're making vanilla pudding tomorrow
With all the best ingredients,
Cinnamon from Sri Lanka
And sweet butter from France!

E Read the sentences. Which action is happening now? Which action will happen in the future?

a We're making vanilla pudding tomorrow.   **b** I'm dreaming about it now.

F **Learn Grammar** Present Continuous for Future Plans

The **present continuous** tense can tell about future actions that someone plans. Include the future time when you use this tense.

I'm making a **special breakfast** today.

Read each sentence. Underline the present continuous tense. Then circle the future time word or words.

1   We're playing soccer after school today.

2   My parents are having dinner at a nice restaurant tomorrow.

3   I'm meeting my friends at the station at 1:00 p.m.

4   Carol and I are baking cookies next week.

> I'm cleaning my bedroom on Saturday morning.

G Make a chart like this one. Then talk to your partner about it.

My Plans This Weekend	When I Will Do Them
clean my bedroom	Saturday morning

Listening

Think What food from plants do you eat? Which one is your favorite and why?

A Listen. Match the food group to two examples. Then fill in the blank with an example that you hear from the list. 🔊 1·33

Food Group	Examples I Heard	
1 whole grains ●	● **a** spinach, broccoli, _____	black beans
2 vegetables ●	● **b** soybeans, chickpeas, _____	carrots
3 fruits ●	● **c** almonds, flaxseeds, _____	oranges
4 beans ●	● **d** bread, spaghetti, **rice** _____	pecans
5 nuts and seeds ●	● **e** apples, blueberries, _____	~~rice~~

B Listen again. Fill in the chart. 🔊 1·34

Food Group	1 whole grains	2 vegetables	3 fruits	4 beans	5 nuts and seeds
Percentage of Food	35%				

Speaking 🔊 1·35

C **Learn** Giving a Reason for a Preference

Give a reason why you prefer one thing to another.

I like oranges, but I prefer **bananas** because **they are easier to peel.**

Think of two similar foods that you like. Which do you prefer and why? Tell your partner.

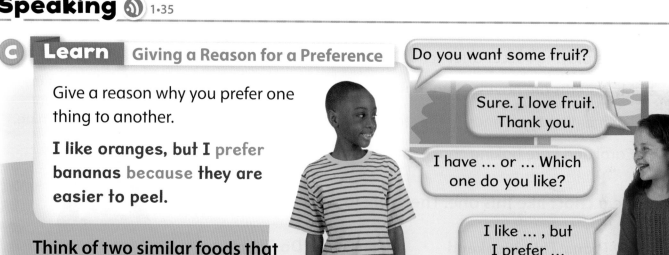

Do you want some fruit?

Sure. I love fruit. Thank you.

I have ... or ... Which one do you like?

I like ... , but I prefer ... because ... What about you?

Word Study

D | Learn | Phrasal Verbs with *Drop*

Some phrasal verbs begin with the verb **drop** and are followed by a preposition.

The farmer dropped off her vegetables at the market.

Listen and read the words. Circle the prepositions. Then write sentences using phrasal verbs with *drop* in your notebook. 🔊 1·36

drop off	drop by	drop back	drop out

A–Z

Writing Study

E | Learn | Interesting Adjectives

Interesting adjectives can improve your writing. Compare the sentences below.

My chickens lay good eggs.
My chickens lay wonderful eggs.

Wonderful is a more interesting adjective than *good*. Interesting adjectives can help you describe your ideas clearly in your writing.

Underline the adjective in each sentence. Then choose a more interesting adjective from each set. Talk about your choices with your partner.

1 The crash in the kitchen was so loud.   noisy   bad

2 Timmy was scared of the thunder outside.   afraid   fearful

3 Miguel did not like the cold weather.   freezing   cool

 Write Now practice writing in the **Workbook.** page 47 ▷

BIG QUESTION ③

Where does our food come from?

Food comes from different countries around the world.

Some food grows on plantations.

Words

A Listen and say the words. Then read and listen to the sentences. 🔊 1·37

convenient	export	local	process	package	farmer's market

agriculture	corporate farm	decrease	century	chemical

1 Cooking food in a microwave oven is **convenient**.

2 Some countries **export** fruits to other countries.

3 The **local** supermarket is a good place to meet people.

4 Companies **process** apples into apple juice.

5 Workers **package** food and send it to supermarkets.

6 My family visits the **farmer's market** in the summer.

7 Modern **agriculture** helps people have enough food.

8 A **corporate farm** has big machines and many workers.

9 Some people want the distance their food travels to **decrease**.

10 Many changes happened in farming in the last **century**.

11 Some **chemicals** are bad for people and animals.

B Two of the three words are correct. Cross out the wrong answer.

1 People may do this to food before they sell it.   local   process   package

2 We can get food from this place.   farmer's market   century   corporate farm

3 This describes some food in a supermarket.   local   convenient   decrease

4 This is a way to provide food for people.   agriculture   export   convenient

C Complete the sentences with the correct words below.

chemicals   century   export

A _____ ago, farmers used very few _____ on their crops.

Countries didn't _____ as much food as they do now either.

Before You Read

 Think What animals and plants do farmers raise and grow in your area?

From the World to Your Table

In this *informational text*, you will read about how far food travels to feed people around the world. Informational texts are full of facts and ideas about a subject. As you read, summarize the main ideas.

Social Studies: Geography

D **Learn** Summarize

Summarize a reading to show that you understand it. You can summarize a reading in two steps:

1 Find the most important ideas and details in the reading.

2 Briefly rewrite these ideas in your own words.

Read each paragraph. Then summarize the paragraph in one or two sentences.

1

> Are you cooking squash for dinner? There are many kinds. Acorn squash is round and sweet. Banana squash is long. However, it doesn't taste anything at all like a banana!

<u>There are many kinds of squash with different shapes</u>

<u>and tastes.</u>

2

> If you feel sick, have some broccoli. This short, green plant is part of the cabbage family. Broccoli is full of vitamins and has calcium, just like milk! Many people call broccoli a "superfood."

_____

_____

E **Words in Context** Scan the reading on pages 58–59 and circle these words. As you read, guess what they mean.

grocery stores	food labels	organic food	whole food

F Scan the reading for country names. What country names can you find? What do you know about food from these countries?

From the World to

The next time you eat dinner, look closely at the food on your plate. If you are eating in the summertime, it's possible that some of the food comes from your own garden. Some might come from the local farmer's market. However, most of your food probably comes from far away.

For centuries, people grew their own food and ate it themselves, keeping some for the long winter. In some countries, people continue to do this. However, agriculture has changed a great deal in the last 100 years. Most people no longer grow their own food. They buy it in supermarkets and grocery stores. Some of the food they buy comes from small family farms, but much of it comes from large corporate farms. Companies process and package most of this food before it gets to the supermarket.

For example, they make orange juice from oranges. They also make flour from wheat, and then they make bread from the flour!

Would you like to know where your food comes from? You can check yourself. Most food labels give this information. You may be surprised at what you discover. The map below gives just a few examples of countries that export food to places around the world.

Thanks to modern agriculture, people around the world can enjoy apples from South Africa, pineapples from Costa Rica, and tomatoes from Mexico. They can eat pasta from Italy, kimchi from Korea, and cheese from Holland. They can enjoy this food without traveling to these places. Instead, the food travels to them.

Think
Summarize what you just read in one or two sentences.

Common Food Exports

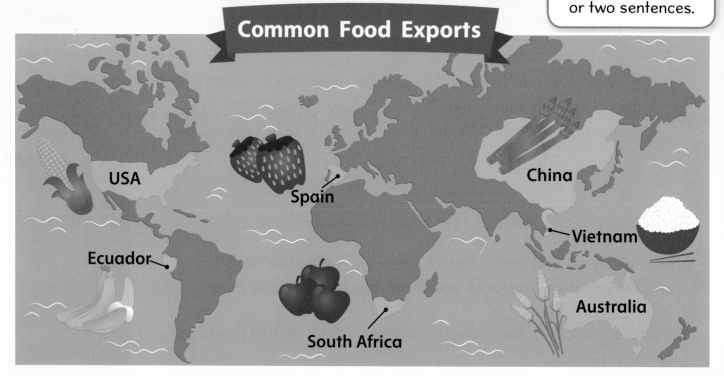

USA

Spain

China

Vietnam

Ecuador

Australia

South Africa

Your Table

Japan

5,900 MILES
9,300 KM

New Zealand

"Food miles" is the distance that food travels to get to us. For example, a person who lives in Japan may buy kiwifruit that comes from New Zealand. This kiwifruit has to travel 5,800 miles (9,300 kilometers) to get to this person. Airplanes, ships, trains, and trucks may bring this food. This transportation uses a lot of fuel that can cause pollution. When food travels, some of it needs to stay cool, which takes more energy and fuel. Also, companies put chemicals on food to help it last longer while it travels. These chemicals may not be good for our health.

In our modern world, most people can't grow all the food they need. However, there are four things you can do to help decrease energy and keep food healthy and delicious:

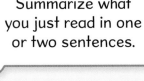

Think
Summarize what you just read in one or two sentences.

1. **Buy food that farmers grow in your area.**

2. **Buy organic food, which doesn't have chemicals on it.**

3. **Buy whole food with less processing and packaging.**

4. **Try to grow more of your own food!**

It's convenient to buy food from all around the word. However, there may be farmers very close to you who grow the same food. By choosing local food, you can save energy, improve your health, and help local businesses. As people say, "Eat locally, think globally!"

Think
Summarize the entire article in three or four sentences.

Comprehension

 Think How does this reading change the way you look at food? Tell your partner three ways you think differently now.

A Summarize three problems caused by eating food from far away. Then summarize the solutions to these problems.

Problems	Solutions
1 Food transportation can cause pollution.	
2	
3	

B Answer the questions.

1 What is a quick way to find out where food in a supermarket comes from?

2 Why don't people have to travel to other countries to get the food they want?

3 Why is buying food from local farmers a good idea?

C **Words in Context** Match each phrase to a picture.

1 grocery store   2 food labels   3 organic food   4 whole food

a

b

c

d

Grammar in Use

D Listen and read along. 🔊 1·39

Would you like to try my cheesecake? / Of course!

Would you like strawberries on top? They're from Spain! / Sure!

Would you like me to call Harry? There are two more pieces.

Harry? Who's Harry?

E Read the sentences. Which one asks about an action? Which one asks about a thing?

a Would you like strawberries on top?   **b** Would you like me to call Harry?

F **Learn Grammar** Polite Offers

Use *Would you like … ?* to make a **polite offer**. You can use this phrase to offer an action or a thing.

Would you like <u>to know</u> where your food comes from? (action)

Would you like <u>a delicious apple</u> from South Africa? (thing)

Circle the correct answer.

1 Would you like **to** / **a** banana for a snack?

2 Would you like **to** / **a** bake a cake with me?

3 Would you like **to** / **a** piece of pizza?

Would you like a piece of apple pie?

G What is something you would like? What is something you would like to do? Make a chart like this one. Then make polite offers to your partner.

Something I would like	Something I would like to do
a piece of apple pie	

Communicate

Listening

Think Why is it important to find new ways to grow food?

A Listen. Match each type of farming to two reasons why it is good. 1·40

a It doesn't need soil.

1 Terraced Farming

b It keeps buildings cooler.

c The soil doesn't wash away.

2 Hydroponic Farming

d Fewer trucks are needed in the city.

e Plants need less water to grow.

3 Rooftop Farming

f It's good for plants that need lots of water.

B Listen again. Then circle the correct answer. 1·41

1 Which type of farming is the lettuce farm in Belgium?
terraced   hydroponic   rooftop

2 Which type of farming is the rice farm in Vietnam?
terraced   hydroponic   rooftop

3 Which type of farming is the vegetable farm in Hong Kong?
terraced   hydroponic   rooftop

Speaking 1·42

C What vegetables or fruits do people grow in your area? Talk to your partner about these vegetables or fruits and two dishes made with them.

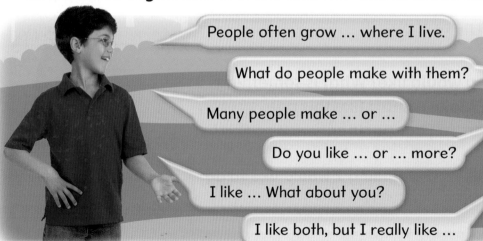

People often grow ... where I live.

What do people make with them?

Many people make ... or ...

Do you like ... or ... more?

I like ... What about you?

I like both, but I really like ...

Word Study

D **Learn** Four-syllable Words

Large words can have many **syllables**. You can hear the syllables in a word more clearly if you say the word slowly. When you say the word normally, the syllables blend together.

Agriculture has changed a great deal in the last 100 years.

If you say *agriculture* slowly, it sounds like *ag-ri-cul-ture*.

Listen. Repeat each word slowly and then normally. Then write each word divided into syllables. Use your dictionary to help you. 1·43

introduction	dictionary	environment	geography	conversation	photographer

A-Z

1 introduction   **in-tro-duc-tion**

2 dictionary   _____

3 environment   _____

4 geography   _____

5 conversation   _____

6 photographer   _____

Writing Study

E **Learn** Prepositional Phrases of Location

Prepositional phrases of location tell where something is. They include a preposition and its object. The object is a noun or a pronoun.

The garden is behind the house.
prep.   object

The asparagus is near the carrots.
prep.   object

Read each sentence. Underline the prepositional phrase of location.

1 The rice is <u>between the green beans and the soup</u>.

2 The chocolate chip cookies are on the shelf.

3 The flower bulbs are under the ground all winter.

4 The potato plants are next to the tomato plants.

 Write Now practice writing in the **Workbook**. page 55

Wrap Up

Writing

A Read this research report about where food comes from.

Title —— **The Food on Your Plate**

Introduction —— Look at the food on your plate. Each food probably comes from a different place. When my mom made lasagna last week, I learned a lot about where food comes from.

Body ——
As my mom prepared the ingredients, I looked at all of the labels. I discovered that the pasta and canned tomatoes came from Italy, and the eggplant came from Mexico. In fact, all of the vegetables were from other countries except for the zucchini. My grandmother grew it in her garden!

I asked my mom about spices. She showed me an interesting book about them. My mom uses salt from China and black pepper from Vietnam. The book explained that China and the United States produce 40 percent of the world's salt, and Vietnam exports more black pepper than any other country.

Finally, I wanted to know about the sauce, so I looked up the sauce company on the Internet. They make it right here in our city!

Conclusion ——
As you can see, our food comes from many different places. Hopefully I can visit all of these places someday. That would certainly be a world tour!

B Answer the questions.

1   What two foods in the lasagna came from places near the writer?
2   What are some of the countries that the ingredients came from?
3   Where did the writer find information about the ingredients?

Learn Research Report

- Get information from books, people, and the Internet. This information is your research.
- Write an introduction that includes your main idea.
- Write paragraphs using your research. Each paragraph should have details and examples that support your main idea.
- Write a conclusion that summarizes your research in an interesting way.

 Write Now go to the **Workbook** to plan and write your own report. page 56

Project: Creating a Story

C **Create a story about food from around the world.**

- In your group, read your research reports aloud.

- Talk about what you like about each report. Then choose one report. Your group will write a fictional story about it. Look at "The Breakfast Quest" for ideas on how to write your story.

- Give your story a title. Then plan the characters, the ingredients, and where the ingredients come from.

- Draw pictures of the ingredients in your story. Write down words you want to remember on the back of the pictures.

- Choose who will present each part of the story or who will be each character.

- Practice telling your story with your group.

- Tell your story to the class. Show your drawings, make eye contact, and speak loudly and clearly.

> We're going on a fruit salad adventure!

> First we'll swim to Chile for kiwifruit.

> Then we'll sail to Papua New Guinea for the best bananas.

> Off we go in a plane to Morocco! We'll get prickly pear fruit.

BIG QUESTION 3

Where does our food come from?

A Watch the video.

B Think more about the Big Question. What did you learn?

C Complete the **Big Question Chart.**

> What did you learn about where food comes from?

In units **7** and **8** you will:

WATCH a video about art and artists.

LEARN about the reasons artists create art.

READ about real artists and a boy who loves art.

BIG QUESTION 4

Why do we make art?

A Watch the video. ▶

B Look at the picture and talk about it.

1 Where are the girls? What do you see in this place?

2 What are they doing? What are they using to do this?

C Think and answer the questions.

1 What kind of art do you make at school?

2 How is art class different from science class?

D Fill out the **Big Question Chart**.

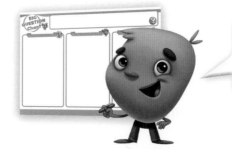

What do you know about art? What do you want to know?

Words

A Listen and read the words. Listen again and say the words. 🔊 2·02

    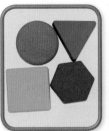 

sketch	pastels	canvas	paintbrushes	shapes	string

three-dimensional	prodigy	street painter	carpenter	sculptor

B Circle True (T) or False (F).

1   You can tie things together with string.   **T**   **F**
2   Circles, squares, and triangles are shapes.   **T**   **F**
3   A prodigy is usually an adult person.   **T**   **F**
4   A photograph is three-dimensional.   **T**   **F**
5   You need paint to make a sketch.   **T**   **F**
6   Carpenters work with clay.   **T**   **F**
7   Street painters work outdoors.   **T**   **F**
8   Paintbrushes only come in one size.   **T**   **F**

C Three of the four words are correct. Cross out the wrong answer.

1   This person creates something new.
     street painter   shapes   carpenter   sculptor

2   Artists use these things to make art.
     pastels   paintbrushes   sketches   canvases

Before You Read

Think What art have you seen? How did you feel about it?

D **Learn** Text Features

Text features can help you understand the information in a reading. These features include:

Title	what the reading is about
Heading	what a part of the reading is about
Visual	a photograph or an illustration
Caption	words under or near a visual

Label the text features of the reading below using the following words. You will use one word twice.

> caption   title   visual   heading

1 _____

2 _____

3 _____

4 _____

5 _____

The Beauty of Recycled Art ❶

A Creative New Art Form ❷

Recycled art is very popular. Artists make recycled art from trash. They use old lamps, bicycles, and even chewing gum!

An Earth-Friendly Art Form ❸ ❹

Recycled art is creative and friendly to the Earth. Artists recycle old and unwanted objects. This uses less energy and fewer materials. It teaches people to be less wasteful.

❺ This is a table that uses recycled materials.

E **Words in Context** Scan the reading on pages 70–71 and circle these words. As you read, guess what the words mean.

> complex   washable   combines   fascination

F Look at the text features in the article. What do you now know before you start reading?

Art Through New Eyes

In this *magazine article*, you will read about four exciting modern artists and the art they create. A magazine article gives information and often uses text features. As you read, use the text features to help you understand more about the article.

Art

Art Through New Eyes

Think

How does the title help you understand the reading?

Can anyone make art? Can artists make art from anything? Let's look at art through the eyes of some very inspiring modern artists to answer these questions.

The Painting Prodigy

Although he is busy with school and football, Kieron draws or paints daily.

Sailing on the Broads shows Kieron's love of the sea.

When he was five, Kieron Williamson drew sketches of boats he saw on a family trip to Cornwall, England. This was the start of Kieron's love of drawing. The more he drew, the more complex his drawings became. Kieron wanted to learn more about art, so he spent time with local artists in his hometown of Norfolk, England. They helped him build his skills in drawing and painting. He now creates pictures using oil paints, pastels, and watercolors. Today, nine-year-old Kieron is considered to be a child prodigy. Around the world, people admire his beautiful artwork, including many famous people. The young artist says, "I like creating art because it's fun and inspiring. It makes me think of places I can't see."

When people step onto one of Mueller's paintings, like *The Crevasse*, they become part of it.

Art Under Your Feet

The next time you walk outside, you may discover that you are part of Edgar Mueller's art. Edgar is an expert street painter from Germany. "I always have the wish to create something new," he says. You can find his paintings all around the world at festivals and on public walkways. His three-dimensional paintings include waterfalls, canyons, and more. Mueller uses washable paint or chalk, a variety of paintbrushes, and string. His work helps people to look at a place differently.

"I absolutely fell in love with painting on the street," Mueller says.

Think

How does the heading above help you understand the paragraph?

Stick Sculptures

Patrick Dougherty is a unique sculptor. He combines his love of nature with his skills as a carpenter. His goal is "to build a great sculpture that excites people's imaginations." You can see his large-scale sculptures in many places around the world.

Dougherty's sculptures are made of young trees, or saplings. The saplings are flexible, so he can bend them into rounded shapes. He keeps them together by weaving the saplings around each other. Building the sculpture is a big job, so the local community helps Dougherty with his project. Many volunteers help to collect the saplings, mark out the space, and build the sculpture. The sculptures are temporary. They will decompose, or break down, over time.

Dougherty creates large-scale sculptures like *Call of the Wild.*

"Sticks are something we all have in common," Dougherty says.

Painting the Universe

When you look at the artwork of Korean artist Sung Hee Cho up close, you see small pieces of brightly colored paper on a large canvas. It may seem disorderly with colors scattered around. However, as you step back, you can imagine the stars, galaxies, and the beauty of the universe. Cho combines *hanji*, traditional Korean paper, with paint. First, she paints the canvas. Then, she cuts out pieces of *hanji* into small shapes, such as flower petals. Next, she dyes and paints the small pieces of paper in a different color. Then she glues thousands of them onto the canvas in layers to capture the glimmer of light. She repeats this process over and over again. She wants to create artwork that is as magical as stars.

By carefully observing the stars, Cho created *The Star in the Cosmos.*

Think

How do the photos and captions in this section help you to understand Sung Hee Cho's art?

Cho wants to share her fascination with the universe through her artwork.

Inspiring artists come from every part of the world. Each one inspires us in a different way. By creating and sharing their art, they help us appreciate and understand the world around us.

Comprehension

 Think Which artist would you like to talk to? What questions would you ask him or her?

A Match a heading to an artist. Then match an artist to a sentence.

1 The Painting ● Prodigy

● **a** Edgar Mueller ●

● **e** People can walk on this artist's paintings.

2 Art Under ● Your Feet

● **b** Sung Hee Cho ●

● **f** This artist is interested in the universe.

3 Stick ● Sculptures

● **c** Kieron Williamson ●

● **g** This artist makes art from natural things.

4 Painting the ● Universe

● **d** Patrick Dougherty ●

● **h** This artist is very young, but he's a skilled painter.

B Answer the questions.

1 Who helped Kieron Williamson build his skills?

2 How do people become a part of an Edgar Mueller painting?

3 Who helps Patrick Dougherty build his sculptures?

4 What is the Korean name for the paper Sung Hee Cho uses?

C **Words in Context** Complete each sentence with a word from the box.

complex   washable   combines   fascination

1 The artist _____ blue and yellow paint to make green paint.

2 Many artists have a _____ with nature.

3 Jackie spilled paint on her sweater, but the paint is _____.

4 Sara's sketch is more _____ than Ronald's.

Grammar in Use

D Listen and sing along. **Be an Artist** 🔊 2·04

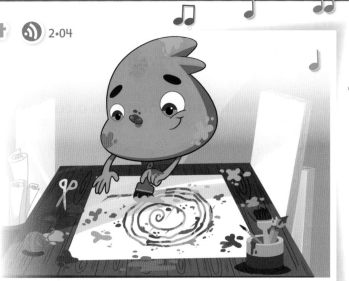

Anyone can be an artist
And make art from anything.
Let's make something beautiful
With just a ball of string!

Glue the string in a circle.
Add a head and a tail.
Paint it yellow, blue, and green.
Now it's a beautiful snail!

E Read the sentences. Which one names a person? Which one doesn't?

a Amy can be an artist.   **b** Anyone can be an artist.

F **Learn Grammar** Indefinite Pronouns

Use **indefinite pronouns** to talk about unnamed people or things.

Can anyone make art? (any of the people)
I want to paint something in this room. (one of the things)
Everyone worked on the sculpture. (all of the people)

Circle the correct indefinite pronoun in each sentence.

1 There is **something** / **anything** I like about this sculpture.

2 Did you meet **everything** / **anyone** at the art gallery?

3 The art teacher helps **everyone** / **someone** with their drawings.

G Make a chart like the one below. Write down the names of people and items in your classroom. Ask your partner to guess what you wrote.

I'm thinking of someone with a green pencil case.

Is it Daniel?

People	Items
Daniel	the teacher's desk

Grammar: Indefinite Pronouns **Unit 7** **73**

Communicate

Listening

 Think What is your favorite type of art to create? Why do you create it?

A Listen. Match each name to a country and a type of art. 🎧 2·05

1	Stella	•	•	**a**	Paraguay	•	•	**e**	photography
2	Juan	•	•	**b**	Tanzania	•	•	**f**	Sami jewelry
3	Neema	•	•	**c**	Croatia	•	•	**g**	computer art
4	Marko	•	•	**d**	Sweden	•	•	**h**	junk art

B Listen again. Write the correct artist beside each reason. 🎧 2·06

	Reason for Creating Art	**Artist**
1	I capture the magic of things. It's like a treasure hunt.	_____
2	We relax together and continue our family tradition.	_____
3	I want to make a difference, and I like being creative.	_____
4	I challenge myself and let my imagination soar.	_____

Speaking 🎧 2·07

C Ask and answer questions about the picture with your partner. Use short answers.

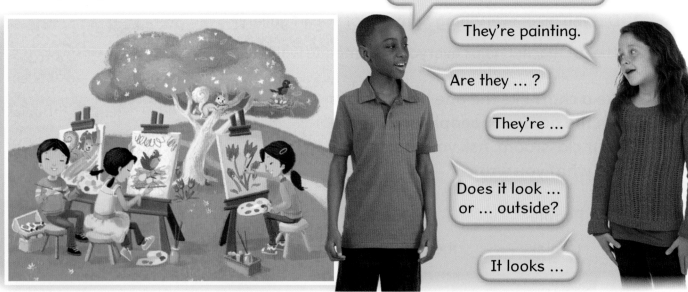

What are the children doing?

They're painting.

Are they … ?

They're …

Does it look … or … outside?

It looks …

Word Study

D **Learn** Words with the Prefix *dis-*

The prefix **dis-** means *not* or *the opposite of*.

The artist's studio was messy and disorganized.

Listen and read the words. Circle the prefixes. Then write a sentence for each word in your notebook. 🔊 2·08

| dissatisfied | disorganized | dishonest | disprove | disability | distrust |

Writing Study

E **Learn** Compound Predicate

A predicate is the action of a sentence. A **compound predicate** is two or more actions that a subject does. Join the actions with a conjunction, such as *and*.

Picasso painted many masterpieces. He created many sculptures.
     predicate   predicate

Picasso painted many masterpieces and created many sculptures.
                    compound predicate

Read each pair of sentences. Then combine them into one sentence.

1 We put away the paint. We washed our hands.

_____

2 The artist talked to the students. She showed them her paintings.

_____

3 The artist found simple materials. He made sculptures with them.

_____

 Now practice writing in the **Workbook.** page 66

BIG QUESTION 4

Why do we make art?

We make art because it's fun.

Art helps us to look at things in a new way.

Words

A Listen and say the words. Then read and listen to the sentences. 🔊 2·09

exhibition	frame	landscape	texture	shading

perspective	contrast	space	stained	brilliant	pale

1   There is an **exhibition** of student art at school today.

2   Kara put a wooden **frame** around her painting.

3   The **landscape** showed tall mountains and a river.

4   David uses paper and cloth to give his paintings **texture**.

5   The **shading** in this sketch makes the animal look real.

6   The drawing's **perspective** made the streets look very long.

7   A black and white painting has a lot of **contrast**.

8   The small objects in the painting had empty **space** between them.

9   Paula's apron was **stained** with many colors of paint.

10   The artist painted the dragonfly with **brilliant** green wings.

11   The mountains looked **pale** and gray under the cloudy sky.

B Match each item or group of items to the correct word.

1   the sunset　　　　•　　• **a**　stained

2   an artist's hands　•　　• **b**　pale

3   a sick child's face　•　　• **c**　brilliant

4   sculptures　•　　• **d**　exhibition

5   lakes, forests　•　　• **e**　frame

6   wood, metal　•　　• **f**　landscape

C Read each quote. Then write what the quote is about.

1   "The surface of the painting is thick and bumpy." This is about ____**texture**____.

2   "The yellow looks brighter next to the purple." This is about _____.

3   "The bird in the painting is alone in the vast sky." This is about _____.

4   "The light and dark lines make the apple look real." This is about _____.

5   "The mountains look far away in the painting." This is about _____.

Before You Read

 Think What do you want to be when you are older? Why? Do you think you will be able to be this? Why or why not?

D **Learn** | Value Judgments |

> A **value judgment** is an opinion about a character and what he or she does. To make a value judgment as you read, ask yourself, *What kind of person is this character? Did he or she do the right thing? Did he or she make the right decision?*

Read the paragraphs. Choose a value judgment.

1

> Kelly was out of paint. She looked around the empty art studio. All the other artists were gone. Kelly really wanted to finish her painting. She quickly opened Steve's desk, grabbed some paint, and took it back to her canvas.

    a Kelly did the right thing. She didn't need to ask Steve to borrow his paint.
    b Kelly didn't do the right thing. She needed to ask Steve to use his paint.

2

> George had to get to art class on time. He ran through the park and came to a traffic light. A little boy was waiting there with his mother. The light was red, but there were no cars coming. George waited until the light turned green, and he was late for class.

    a George didn't do the right thing. He shouldn't be late for class.
    b George did the right thing. The little boy was watching him.

E **Words in Context** Scan the story on pages 78–79 and circle these words. As you read, guess what the words mean.

| ignore | worries | famous | speechless |

F Why do people go to art galleries? Tell your partner the reasons you think of.

Sketches in a Gallery

In this *realistic fiction* story, a boy who loves art meets someone special in a gallery. A realistic fiction story has characters, problems, and settings that seem real. As you read, stop and make value judgments.

Elizabeth Cody Kimmel is the author of over 30 children's books. She lives in New York City.

Read 🔊 2·10

Think

What value judgments can you make about Theo?

Sketches

Each day after school when other boys play soccer, practice for the school play, or ride bikes, Theo goes to the art museum. Everyone he knows thinks this is strange, even his own family.

"Don't you want to play a sport or be in the play with all of your friends? I will sign you up for something," his mother offers.

Theo does not tell his mother that he has no friends at school. His friends are all here in the museum. They are on every wall, in brilliant colors and oil paints and pastels. The paintings are Theo's friends. Today, Theo rushes to get to the museum after school because he will be meeting some new friends. An exhibition is opening—The Mountain Landscapes of Zayan Khan.

Inside the brightly lit gallery, there are ten new paintings, each in a wooden frame. Each painting features a different mountain. Some of the mountains are covered in snow, while others are green or rocky. Theo sits on a bench and looks at one painting for a very long time. He likes the contrast of the heavy black lines of the mountain and the pale blue sky. Theo takes out his notebook and his pencil and begins to make a sketch.

People come and go from the small gallery, but Theo sits for a long time, making sketch after sketch. After a while, there is only one other person left in the gallery. He is sitting on a bench on the other side of the little room.

Theo decides to ignore the man. I don't want to talk to him, Theo thinks.

The man stands and walks toward the exit, but he stops next to Theo.

Theo's sketch is of a mountain from very far away. The mountain is small and surrounded by space.

in a Gallery

"That's an interesting perspective," the man comments.

Theo is shocked. He never shows his artwork to anyone because he worries that it isn't any good.

"Shall I show you some more sketches?" he asks.

The man smiles and nods. Theo hands the man his notebook and sits quietly as the man turns the pages.

"I like the way you create texture with shading," the man remarks. "I like to do that, too."

Theo notices the man's hands and fingers are stained with paint. In his jacket pocket, there are several colored pencils and a paintbrush. He is holding an old, tattered sketchbook with his name written on the front.

"You are Zayan Kahn!" Theo exclaims, astounded that he is talking to the famous artist. Zayan Kahn looks so much younger than Theo imagined, and he is so kind and friendly.

"That's right," Zayan Kahn replies.

"I'm Theo. One day, I want to be an artist like you," Theo tells him.

Zayan Kahn shakes his head. "No, don't say that," he says.

Theo looks down. "Oh," he says.

Zayan Kahn points to Theo's notebook.

"You are already an artist, Theo," he says.

Theo is speechless with happiness. He does not say anything else, and neither does Zayan Kahn. They just sit quietly in the room, sketching, two artists surrounded by friends.

Think

What value judgments can you make about Theo and Zayan Khan?

79

Understand

Comprehension

 How do you feel about Theo? Are you similar to him? Why or why not? Tell your partner two opinions you have about Theo.

A Read each value judgment. Circle A if you agree. Circle D if you disagree. Talk about your choices with your partner.

1 Theo should try to make more friends at school. **A** **D**

2 Theo shouldn't go to the art museum so often. **A** **D**

3 It is good that Theo sketches other people's art. **A** **D**

4 Theo should ignore the man in the gallery. **A** **D**

5 Zayan Khan is a kind man. **A** **D**

6 Theo and Zayan Khan are similar. **A** **D**

B Answer the questions.

1 What would Theo's mother like him to do?

2 How would you describe Zayan Khan's landscapes?

3 Why doesn't Theo usually show his sketches to anyone?

4 Why are Theo and Zayan Khan silent at the end of the story?

C **Words in Context** Match each word to a picture.

1 ignore 2 famous 3 worries 4 speechless

a

b

c

d

Grammar in Use

D Listen and read along. 🔊 2•11

E Read each sentence. What is the speaker offering in each sentence?

a I'll bring you ice cream.　　**b** Shall I frame it?

F **Learn Grammar**　Offers with *Shall* and *Will*

> Use **shall** to make an offer with a question.
>
> "**Shall** I show you some more sketches?" he asks.
>
> Use **will** to make an offer with a statement.
>
> "I **will** sign you up for something," his mother offers.

Match each situation on the left with an offer on the right.
Write the correct letter.

1 A woman has a heavy bag. _____	**a** "I'll get it down."
2 A man is very thirsty. _____	**b** "I'll carry that for you."
3 A child's kite is in a tree. _____	**c** "Shall I bring you a cold drink?"

G Make a chart like the one below. Write actions and offer them to your partner.

> You look cold. Shall I close the window?

Shall I ... ?	I will ...
close the window	

Listening

Think In nature, where can you see many colors mixed together?

A Compare Impressionist and traditional paintings. Listen and check (✓). 🔊 2·12

	Outdoors	Indoors	More detail	Less detail	Side by side colors	Mixed colors
Impressionist Paintings						
Traditional Paintings						

B Listen again. Answer the questions. 🔊 2·13

1 Where is the Marmottan Monet Museum located?

_____

2 How many works of art by Claude Monet does the museum have?

_____

3 When was *Impression: Sunrise* painted?

_____

Speaking 🔊 2·14

C **Learn** Expressing a Desire or Wish

The verb **wish** can be used to talk about something you want to *do*, *be*, or *have*, but cannot at this time.

I **wish** I could paint like Claude Monet.
I **wish** I were a famous painter.
I **wish** I had more time to paint.

Do you have a wish? Talk to your partner about it.

I wish I could go to Berlin.

Why do you want … ?

I want to …

That sounds fun. I wish I …

Word Study

D Learn Synonyms

Remember, **synonyms** are words that have similar meanings.

They are on every wall in brilliant **colors.**
They are on every wall in bright **colors.**

Listen and read the words. Then match the sentences with synonyms. 🔊 2·15

beautiful	gifted	drab	pretty	talented	dreary

A-Z

1 Manuela thought the painting was *beautiful*. ●   ● **a** Everyone agreed that it was very *dreary*.

2 The sky outside looked *drab* and gray. ●   ● **b** Many of her teachers felt that she was very *gifted*.

3 Damla was a *talented* art student. ●   ● **c** Her son thought it was *pretty*, too.

Writing Study

E Learn The Articles *A, An,* and *The*

Use **a** or **an** before a noun if the noun is one of many.
Use **the** before a noun if the noun names one special, or specific, thing.

Theo went to see an **exhibition.**
(There are many exhibitions. Theo went to see one of them.)

Theo went to see the **exhibition of Zayan Khan's landscapes.**
(This exhibition is special because it is Zayan Khan's exhibition.)

Read the sentences. Circle the correct article.

1 **A / The** *Mona Lisa* is Leonardo da Vinci's most famous work of art.

2 I saw **a / the** sculpture at the Chinese sculpture exhibition yesterday.

3 **An / The** art of Vincent van Gogh is different from any other art I've seen.

4 I went to **an / the** art gallery in Paris when I was there.

 Write Now practice writing in the **Workbook**. page 74

Writing

A Read this opinion essay about the writer's favorite work of art.

Title — **Seurat's Beautiful Dots of Paint**

Topic and opinion — The French artist Georges Seurat created many paintings in his short lifetime. One of my favorites is *A Sunday Afternoon on the Island of La Grande Jatte*. I like this painting for three reasons.

Reasons and details —

First of all, Seurat created this painting in a new style called "pointillism," which uses small dots of paint. By putting two colors next to each other, Seurat could trick the eye to see a third color.

Next, this painting is full of details about French life in the 1880s. There are several women wearing elegant clothes and carrying parasols. One woman is even walking a monkey. Many of the men are dressed up with jackets and hats. I can see dogs running around and children playing. There are boats on the water. It looks like a perfect summer day.

Finally, this painting makes me feel very calm. Even though a park like this could be a noisy place, Seurat makes it feel peaceful. He paints people sitting quietly in the shade. There is a girl sniffing a bouquet of flowers. Throughout the painting, people are relaxing on the cool, green grass and enjoying a beautiful day.

Summary and final thought — Seurat needed two years to finish this beautiful painting. I'm grateful that he completed it. It is a very special painting because of Seurat's use of pointillism, his attention to detail, and the calm feeling he created. It is easy to see why so many people admire this painting. I hope that you can see its beauty, too.

B Answer the questions.

1 How does Seurat's pointillism style trick the eye?
2 What unusual animal can the writer see in this painting?
3 How does this painting make the writer feel calm?

Learn Opinion Essay

- In the introduction paragraph, present the topic and write your opinion.
- In the three body paragraphs, write the reasons why you have your opinion. Be sure to include details that support your reasons.
- In the conclusion paragraph, give a brief summary of your reasons. Then write an interesting final thought.

Write Now go to the **Workbook** to plan and write your own opinion essay. page 75

Project: Acting in a Play

C Create a short play about artists working in a studio. Then act it out.

- In your group, create a play about artists in a studio.

- Think about different types of art, what artists do, and what kind of artist you want to be in the play. Give yourself a unique name and choose what tools you will need.

- Create a drawing of a piece of art. It can be any type of art.

- Think about what artists would say to each other in a studio. Talk about your ideas with your group. Write down words that you want to remember. Then practice the play with your group.

- Perform the play for your class. Remember to speak clearly, show the artwork you created, and act like you are a real artist.

Can I borrow some of your paint? I ran out of mine!

I have lots of paint! Which colors do you need?

I'm sorry. I only have a little bit left, and I need to finish this portrait.

BIG QUESTION 4

Why do we make art?

A Watch the video.

B Think more about the Big Question. What did you learn?

C Complete the **Big Question Chart**.

What did you learn about art?

In units **9** and **10** you will:

WATCH
a video about cities in different places.

LEARN
about the many features of a city.

READ
about Jakarta and a very young mayor.

WRITE a persuasive essay.

CREATE a travel brochure.

BIG QUESTION 5

What is a city?

A Watch the video. ▶

B Look at the picture and talk about it.

1 What do you see in the picture?

2 How is the city similar to and different from where you live?

C Think and answer the questions.

1 What can you do in a city?

2 How are cities different than places that are not cities?

D Fill out the **Big Question Chart**.

What do you know about cities? What do you want to know?

87

Words

A Listen and read the words. Listen again and say the words. 🔊 2•16

canal

port

architecture

rickshaw

street vendor

antiques

souvenirs

batik

exotic fruits

tuna

shrimp

B Write the following words in the correct spaces. Talk to your partner about your answers.

> rickshaw   batik   shrimp   souvenirs   tuna   antiques   exotic fruits

Eat in a City	Ride in a City	Buy in a City

C Circle True (T) or False (F).

1   You can see many ships at a port.   **T   F**

2   Cities usually have only one kind of architecture.   **T   F**

3   Canals are natural and not man-made.   **T   F**

4   You can often buy food from a street vendor.   **T   F**

5   Antiques were made very recently.   **T   F**

Before You Read

 Think What cities around the world do you know about? What do you know about these cities?

D **Learn** | Paraphrasing

You can **paraphrase** what you read by writing it in your own words. This can help you remember main ideas or important facts in a reading.

You read	Shanghai's population is the largest of any city in China.
You paraphrase	Shanghai has more people than any other Chinese city.

Match each sentence with its paraphrased sentence.

Sentence			**Paraphrased Sentence**
1 For centuries, Shanghai was a major trading town.	●	●	**a** Many people travel to Shanghai to see the city.
2 Shanghai is a popular destination for tourists.	●	●	**b** Many ships come into and leave Shanghai.
3 Shanghai is one of the busiest port cities in the world.	●	●	**c** People bought and sold goods in Shanghai for hundreds of years.

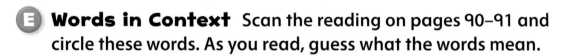

E **Words in Context** Scan the reading on pages 90–91 and circle these words. As you read, guess what the words mean.

> countless   congested   haggle   banned

F Look at the pictures on the following page. What looks interesting to you? What would you like to see in Jakarta?

Reading: Paraphrasing **Unit 9** **89**

Jakarta: A Big-City Snapshot

In this *travel article*, you will tour Jakarta, one of Asia's largest cities. Travel articles describe interesting places and things to do around the world. As you read, paraphrase sentences that contain important facts or information.

Social Studies: Society

Author Patrick Daley enjoys sharing his knowledge of the world with others. He has written books about cities and places in Cuba, Indonesia, Ireland, Kenya, Nigeria, and Russia.

Jakarta:
A Big-City Snapshot

Do you live in a city and have nothing to do? Just step outside! A city has fascinating things to see and interesting places to explore. No one could see everything in one day. This brief look at Jakarta, the capital city of Indonesia, is a good example of what a city has to offer.

Jakarta is a busy port city on the Java Sea. It is filled with more than 10 million people. That's more people than in New York City. Its area is also huge—250 square miles (646 square kilometers).

Think

Paraphrase one of the sentences in the paragraphs above.

This Southeast Asian city stretches high into the sky. Countless skyscrapers give the city a futuristic feel. When you first arrive, it feels like you just stepped off a spaceship.

Jakarta is one of the most congested cities in the world. You might even say they invented the traffic jam. Jakarta is also highly polluted. With so many trains, cars, and motorcycles, it is no wonder.

A VISIT TO THE OLD CITY

Parts of the original Dutch city can still be found in the area called Kota. Kota is located on the north side of the city. It is a great place to wander around. It has old canals and classical architecture.

Top 3 Things To Do in Jakarta

- ✔ Buy chicken curry from a street vendor.
- ✔ People-watch in the fancy "Golden Triangle" shopping district.
- ✔ Take a trip to the top of the Monas, the National Monument of Indonesia.

MODERN CULTURE

Do you want to learn more about the culture of the Indonesian people? Then check out the National Museum. Located in the heart of town, the National Museum is packed with art, historical items, and great displays of Indonesian culture.

You should also head to the Jalan Surabaya antiques market. This is a great spot to pick up souvenirs. You'll find such things as handmade drums, batik-dyed clothing, and jewelry.

The port of Sunda Kelapa is near Kota. Thousands of boats dock here every year. They transport things like coffee, tuna, and exotic fruits.

After watching the ships come and go, check out the Pasar Ikan fish market. It is a great place to inspect strange and exotic fish. It is also a great place to watch people as they shop for dinner and haggle over the price of shrimp.

GETTING AROUND

Indonesia is famous for its rickshaws. These were small, one-passenger carriages that were pulled by a bicycle. Now, they are banned in Jakarta. They were too slow and held up traffic.

They have been replaced by the bajaj, which is a motorized rickshaw. A bajaj is a big seat on wheels pulled around by a moped, a motorized bicycle. Hire a bajaj to take you around the city.

Think
Paraphrase one of the sentences in the paragraphs above.

Think
Paraphrase the final paragraph.

Understand

Comprehension

 Think If you could go to Jakarta for a week, what would you do?
Tell your partner three things you would do and your reasons.

A Write a paraphrased sentence for each sentence below.

1 Indonesia's largest city after Jakarta is Surabaya, with a population of 3 million.

<u>Surabaya has</u> _____

_____

2 Tourists who visit a city often buy souvenirs for their friends and family.

_____

_____

3 Cities offer a variety of restaurants to choose from when you are hungry.

_____

_____

B Answer the questions.

1 Which city has more people, Jakarta or New York City?
2 What makes Jakarta feel like a city from the future?
3 How is Kota different from other parts of Jakarta?
4 What can you do at the Pasar Ikan fish market?
5 Why is a bajaj better than a rickshaw?

C **Words in Context** Match each word to a picture.

1 countless   **2** congested   **3** haggle   **4** banned

a

b

c

d

Grammar in Use

D Listen and sing along. **The Big City** 🔊 2·18

I live in a beautiful busy city.
There is always something fun to do.
There are street vendors selling exotic fruits
And antiques and souvenirs, too.

Nobody's ever bored in the city,
With so many places to go and to see.
The outdoor market, the port, the museum,
Nothing can beat the city for me!

E Read the sentences. Circle the words that begin with *no-*.

a Nobody's ever bored in the city.   **b** Nothing can beat the city for me.

F **Learn Grammar** Negative Indefinite Pronouns

Remember, indefinite pronouns refer to people or objects that we don't
name or know. **Negative indefinite pronouns** begin with *no-*.

Negative Indefinite Pronoun	Meaning	Example
nothing	not anything	**Do you have** nothing **to do?**
no one	no person	No one **could see everything.**
nobody		Nobody **is in the museum.**

Circle the correct negative indefinite pronoun in each sentence.

1 **Nobody / Nothing** can enter the city zoo after 5:00 p.m.
2 There was **no one / nothing** to do at home.
3 **Nobody / Nothing** sat next to me on the bus.

There is nothing
in my pocket.

G Make a chart like this one. Then talk to your partner about it.

There is nothing ...	There is nobody ...
in my pocket	

Communicate

Listening

 Think Is there a body of water in or near your area? What is it? Who uses it?

A **Learn** **Listening for Reasons**

As you hear about things that happened in history, listen for the reasons why those things happened.

Listen. Match a city to its body of water and to a reason the city grew near this water. 🔊 2·19

City	Body of Water	Reason
1 Paris ●	● **a** The Bosphorus ●	● **d** It helped protect people.
2 Mexico City ●	● **b** The River Seine ●	● **e** It provided transportation.
3 Istanbul ●	● **c** Lake Texcoco ●	● **f** It provided food and water.

B Listen again. Answer the questions. 🔊 2·20

1 What does the word "Parisii" mean? _____

2 When did Mexico City begin as an Aztec city? _____

3 Istanbul was the capital city of how many empires? _____

Speaking 🔊 2·21

C Why did your city or town grow where it is today? Think of two possible reasons. Share the reasons with your partner.

My city grew because it is next to a river. The river was important because …

That's really interesting. My city grew because …

How did that help … ?

It helped my city grow because …

Word Study

D **Learn** Words with *Soft c* and *Hard c*

The letter *c* at the beginning of a word can be hard or soft.

A city has fascinating things to see.
    soft c
It has old canals and beautiful architecture.
          hard c

Listen and read the words. Circle the words that begin with a *soft c*. Underline the words that begin with a *hard c*. 2·22

commerce   corner   cinema   cement   castle   ceiling

A-Z

Writing Study

E **Learn** Capitalize the Names of Bodies of Water

Most large bodies of water have names. They begin with capital letters.

River Seine   Lake Texcoco   Pacific Ocean

General words for water, such as *river*, *lake*, and *ocean*, are not capitalized.

Read the paragraph. Capitalize the names of the bodies of water.

>   **D**   **R**
> The danube river is an important river. It flows through many European cities. It's also a trade route. Ships can travel from the danube to the black sea, and then to the sea of marmara. Ships that need to reach an ocean can continue to the indian ocean.

 Now practice writing in the **Workbook.** page 85

BIG QUESTION 5

What is a city?

A city is often near water.

It's an exciting place where many people live and work together.

UNIT 10 — Get Ready

Words

A Listen and say the words. Then read and listen to the sentences. 🔊 2·23

| citizens | volunteers | mayor | assistant | city council | city hall |

| president | garbage collectors | equipment | news conference | playground |

1 The city's **citizens** are happy with the new library.

2 Many **volunteers** cleaned up the town after the storm.

3 The **mayor** spoke to the people of the city.

4 The mayor's **assistant** made phone calls for the mayor.

5 The **city council** discussed the city's schools.

6 At **city hall**, people make decisions about the city.

7 The **president** of our class is a good leader.

8 The **garbage collectors** ride in a huge truck.

9 Workers use heavy **equipment** to fix the city's streets.

10 The reporters asked questions at the **news conference**.

11 Children go to the **playground** after school.

B Circle the correct answer.

1 This person is the head of a city.
    assistant   mayor

2 This person gets paid to do work.
    garbage collector   volunteer

3 You can have fun with your friends here.
    city hall   playground

4 You can learn a lot from watching this.
    equipment   news conference

5 This group of people makes decisions about a city.
    city council   citizens

C Is it easy to be a president? Share your ideas with your partner.

Before You Read

Think What job would you like to have for one day? Why?

D **Learn** Understanding Characters

The **main character** is the person a story is about. The people around the **main character** are the minor characters. As you read about a character, ask yourself:

- **Is this a main character or a minor character?**

- **What strengths and weaknesses does he or she have?**

- **What does this character do and why?**

Read the short story. Answer the questions.

> Every day after school, Antonio and his friend Carlos walked through the park. One day, Antonio lost his cell phone in the park. He offered to help his parents clean the house for one month to pay for a new phone. After a very busy month, Antonio's parents bought him a new phone.

1 Who is the main character? _____

2 Who are the minor characters? _____

3 What strengths and weaknesses does the main character have?

_____

_____

4 Why does the main character work so hard at home?

_____

_____

E **Words in Context** Scan the story on pages 98–99 and circle these words. As you read, guess what they mean.

> contest   ribbon   speech   members

F If you were the mayor, what would you do for the citizens of your city? Why would you do this?

Mayor for a Day

In this *humorous fiction* story, a girl named Marcy discovers what it is like to be the mayor of her city. Humorous fiction stories have characters and events that are funny. As you read, ask yourself about the main character and minor characters in the story. Try to understand what they are like.

Mayor for a Day

Marcy was nervous. She was the winner of the Mayor for a Day contest at her school. For one day, she would be the mayor of her city. Marcy's mother drove her to the Glenview City Hall.

"You'll probably walk around with the mayor," her mother said. "Watch what he does and take notes. You'll learn a lot!"

Outside City Hall, Marcy met Mayor Wilson. To her surprise, he was holding a beach ball.

"Congratulations, Marcy!" he said. "Keep the city running smoothly. You'll work hard, won't you?"

Marcy nodded nervously. "I'll do my best, sir."

Think

Who is the main character? What do you know about her so far?

"Then I'm going to the beach. Mr. Clark will be your assistant today. Goodbye!"

It was a busy morning. Mr. Clark took Marcy to the new city library, which was about to open for the first time. Marcy cut a celebration ribbon and made a short speech. "Citizens of Glenview, read books every day," she declared. "Reading makes you smarter!"

As the crowd clapped, Mr. Clark tapped on his watch. "You have a meeting in ten minutes with the president of the Terrific Toy Company. We want them to build a factory here in Glenview. Many people could get jobs there."

"Let's go," said Marcy.

Think

Who are three minor characters?

In the mayor's office, Marcy spent one hour talking to Hilda Hanson, the president of Terrific Toys. "I promise you that the people of Glenview will build interesting and creative toys," Marcy said.

"For such a young mayor, you impress me!" said Hilda. "We'll start building our factory here tomorrow."

As Hilda drove away, Mr. Clark ran up to Marcy.

"The garbage collectors are unhappy!" he exclaimed. "There is too much garbage to pick up. They want more workers. What will we do?"

Marcy realized that she wasn't nervous anymore. She thought for a moment and then snapped her fingers. "We'll start a recycling program," she said. "That will reduce garbage. They won't need more workers."

"Great idea!" said Mr. Clark.

After lunch, Mr. Clark ran into Marcy's office.

"You have a city council meeting in five minutes!" he shouted.

At the meeting, the head of the city council looked worried. "The playground equipment at the city park needs fresh paint," she said. "The park needs new flowers. But we have no money for extra workers."

"Do we have money for ice cream?" Marcy asked.

The city council members looked confused.

"I will have a news conference today," Marcy explained. "Next Saturday will be our first Glenview Volunteer Day. People can volunteer at the park and enjoy free ice cream. The citizens of our city will paint and plant and get the job done!"

"Wonderful idea, Mayor Marcy!" the members cheered.

At 5:30, Mr. Clark thanked Marcy for her hard work. They walked to the front of City Hall, where Marcy's mother was waiting. Marcy got in the car and stretched her legs.

"Did you have fun, Marcy?" asked her mother.

"I did," said Marcy.

"Who knows?" said her mother. "Maybe you'll be a real mayor someday."

Marcy smiled. "Maybe I will," she said.

Think

What do you know about the main and minor characters?

99

Understand

Comprehension

 What did you like about "Mayor for a Day"? Tell your partner three things you liked about the story. Were there any parts that you didn't like?

A Fill in the chart.

"Mayor for a Day" Main Character: _____	
What problems does the character have?	
What is the character's personality like?	
How does the character act in the story?	
What strengths does the character have?	

B Answer the questions.

1 Why do you think Mayor Wilson wanted to go to the beach?
2 Why was Mr. Clark always running?
3 What did the garbage collectors want? Why?
4 Why did the head of the city council look worried?
5 Do you think Marcy's mother knew what Marcy did all day? Why do you think that way?

C **Words in Context** Match each clue to a word. Write the correct letter.

1 If this is too long, listeners may get bored. ____   **a** ribbon

2 This is easy to lose and difficult to win. ____   **b** members

3 These people all have something in common. ____   **c** speech

4 This is soft enough to cut with a pair of scissors. ____   **d** contest

Grammar in Use

D Listen and read along. 🔊 2·25

You're ready for today's test, aren't you? You didn't forget to study last night, did you?

We don't even have the test on our desks yet … and he's already asking us questions!

E Read the sentences. What is the teacher asking about in each one?

a You're ready for the test, aren't you?   **b** You studied, didn't you?

F **Learn Grammar** Tag Questions

In a **tag question**, a statement is turned into a question by adding a *tag* at the end. A tag question always has a *yes* or *no* answer. Tag questions are often used to say things that we think are true, but that we don't know for sure.

You'll work hard, won't you?
⎣_____⎦ ⎣_____⎦
   statement   tag

Marcy wasn't nervous, was she?
⎣_____⎦ ⎣_____⎦
    statement   tag

Match each statement on the left to a tag on the right to create a tag question.

1 Mayors are hard workers.   ●   ● **a** is he?

2 Mr. Clark isn't the mayor,   ●   ● **b** won't she?

3 Hilda Hanson will build a factory, ●   ● **c** aren't they?

G Make a list like the one below. Then ask your partner tag questions.

Ann is the youngest student, isn't she?

Things I think are true
Ann is the youngest student.

Communicate

Listening

Think What do cities have that small towns don't have?

A Listen. Write where each child lives. 🔊 2·26

1 Toshi _____

2 Gaby _____

3 Alina _____

4 Omari _____

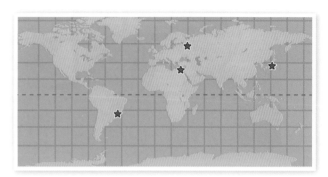

B Listen again. Match each person to a statement. Then circle F for fact or O for opinion. 🔊 2·27

1 Toshi ●	● **a**	You can eat African food in São Paulo.	F	O
2 Gaby ●	● **b**	Pandas are the most beautiful bears.	F	O
3 Alina ●	● **c**	Squash is the most exciting sport.	F	O
4 Omari ●	● **d**	Moscow has almost 100 parks.	F	O

Speaking 🔊 2·28

C **Learn** Asking Questions with *Have To*

Use **have to** to ask about a person's job or duty.

What does a mayor have to **do?**
Do people in your city have to **recycle bottles and cans?**

Ask and answer questions about people's jobs or duties. Use *have to*.

> What does a mayor have to do?

> A mayor has to …

> Does a … have to … ?

> Yes, I think a … has to … / I'm not sure if a … has to …

Word Study

D | Learn | Phrasal Verbs with *Take*

Some phrasal verbs begin with the verb **take**. The past tense of *take* is *took*.

Mayor Wilson took off his glasses. He takes off his glasses often.

Listen and read the words. Then complete the sentences. Change the verb ending and tense if necessary. 🔊 2·29

take down	take in	take after	take over	take up	take apart

1 The girl will _____ the mayor's job for one day.

2 The reading was too long. James couldn't _____ all the information.

3 Samantha _____ the clock, but she couldn't put it back together.

4 Yoon's grandmother _____ knitting last year.

5 On January 1, Alessandro _____ his calendar and put up a new one.

6 Cheryl _____ her mother in many ways.

Writing Study

E | Learn | Coordinating Conjunctions: *And, But, Or*

Use **and**, **but**, and **or** to connect words, phrases, and sentences.

Connect words	**Shannon and Brooke are sisters and friends.**
Connect phrases	**I play chess with my mom but not with my dad.**
Connect sentences	**I can visit you, or you can visit me.**

Read the sentences. Circle the correct coordinating conjunction.

1 I hope to visit Zurich **and** / **but** / **or** Geneva. I want to see both cities.

2 Many cities are much too noisy, **and** / **but** / **or** they are also exciting.

3 Please write a report **and** / **but** / **or** give a speech about cities. Don't do both.

4 I want to go to the city's new library, **and** / **but** / **or** I'm too tired.

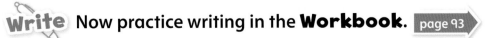

Write Now practice writing in the **Workbook.** page 93 ▷

Writing

A Read this persuasive essay about the writer's city.

Title ——— My City: A Great Place to Live

Introduction ——— Do you live in the countryside? Maybe you live in a small town. If you do, I want to invite you to live in my city. It's a great place to live for many reasons.

Body ———

You may think that a city has too many people. However, people make a city exciting. For example, we have a university right in the center of our city. There are students and teachers everywhere! They go to coffee shops and talk about many interesting things.

Some people say that a city has too many cars and trucks. However, cities also have very good public transportation. My city has taxis, buses, subways, and trains. I go to school every day by subway. It's fast and easy to use.

It is true that cities are not as quiet as towns. However, there are many quiet places in my city. You can rest and enjoy nature in one of our quiet parks. There are many restaurants that have soft music, great service, and delicious food. My city also has a huge library where many people go to read, study, and relax. It's very quiet there.

Conclusion ———

Although cities may have some problems, they also have big rewards. My city is exciting, it has great transportation options, and there are nice quiet areas. Please come and live in my city!

B Answer the questions.

1 Why does the writer include the university in the essay?
2 What are some examples of public transportation?
3 What are some quiet places in a city?

Learn Persuasive Essay

• Include your reason for writing in the introduction paragraph. Your reason should grab your reader's attention.
• In the body paragraphs, first explain how the reader may disagree with you. Then give reasons that will persuade the reader to agree with you.
• Summarize your main ideas in the conclusion paragraph.

 Write Now go to the **Workbook** to plan and write your own persuasive essay. page 94

Project: Creating a Travel Brochure

C **Create a travel brochure that shows interesting parts of your city.**

- In your group, read your persuasive essays to each other. As you listen, make a list of interesting parts of your city. You will create a travel brochure for it!

- Your group should decide which parts of your city you want to include, what you will draw on your brochure, and who will talk about each part.

- Make a plan for how you will share the information in an interesting way.

- Create your travel brochure. Use colorful drawings. You can also use photos of places in your city. You will talk about these places.

- Practice presenting your travel brochure with your group. Write down words you want to remember.

- Present your travel brochure to the class. Remember to hold the brochure so everyone can see it and to speak clearly.

Our city has a river that flows through it. It's a good place to visit on a hot day.

On a rainy day, try seeing one of our city's museums. You can look at art or learn about the history of the city.

Visit the public library. As you can see, it is a beautiful, old building.

BIG QUESTION 5

What is a city?

A **Watch the video.**

B **Think more about the Big Question. What did you learn?**

C **Complete the Big Question Chart.**

What did you learn about cities?

In units **11** and **12** you will:

WATCH
a video about the human body.

LEARN
about many parts of your body.

READ
about a scientist's journey and two body systems.

BIG QUESTION 6

How do our bodies work?

A Watch the video. ▶

B Look at the picture and talk about it.

1 What is the boy doing? What is he using to do this?

2 How do you think the boy feels?

C Think and answer the questions.

1 What parts of the body do you know? What do those parts do?

2 How can you keep your body healthy?

D Fill out the **Big Question Chart**.

What do you know about the human body? What do you want to know?

107

Words

A Listen and say the words. Then read and listen to the sentences. 🔊 2·30

| cells | microscope | virus | bacteria | disease | influenza |

| common cold | mucus | immune | paralyze | infect |

1 Scientists study the body's **cells** to see how they work.

2 Beth uses a **microscope** to see plant cells.

3 A **virus** can enter your body through your nose or mouth.

4 Some **bacteria** can make people very sick.

5 Eating healthy food can protect you from a **disease**.

6 Thomas was in bed for two days with **influenza**.

7 Many students catch the **common cold** every year.

8 A body usually makes more **mucus** when it is sick.

9 Maria can't get the flu because she is **immune** to it.

10 Dr. Butler uses a wheelchair because his legs are **paralyzed**.

11 A sneeze or cough can **infect** another person.

B Two of the three words are correct. Cross out the wrong answer.

1	This is in your body.	cells	microscope	mucus
2	This is always bad for your body.	bacteria	virus	disease
3	You won't feel well if you have this.	common cold	influenza	mucus
4	People don't want their bodies to become this.	immune	paralyzed	infected

C Why do scientists use microscopes? How do microscopes help scientists? Write your ideas. Then share your ideas with your partner.

_____

_____

_____

Before You Read

 Think Did you ever have influenza or a common cold? What happened to your body? How did you feel? Tell your partner three things that happened and how you felt.

D **Learn** Main Idea and Theme

Remember, the **main idea** is what a story is about. You can find the main idea within the words of a story.

The **theme** is a lesson you can learn from the story. Usually, the author does not tell the reader the theme. Use details from the story and your own knowledge to make an inference about the theme.

Read the paragraph. Circle the main idea and theme.

Did you know that the human thumb is very important? Most animals don't have a thumb like a human thumb. Human thumbs are special because we can touch every one of our fingertips with it. Because of this, we can pick up small items, write with a pencil, eat with a spoon or with chopsticks, play instruments, and much more.

1 What is the main idea?
  a Our thumbs let us do many things.

  b We play instruments with our thumbs.

2 What is the theme?
  a Thumbs can touch fingers.

  b The thumb is very special.

E **Words in Context** Scan the story on pages 110–111 and circle these words. As you read, guess what the words mean.

> suit scrape fluid swallowed

F Why do scientists study the human body? If you were a scientist, what would you want to know about the human body? Tell your partner two things you would want to know.

Reading: Main Idea and Theme **Unit 11** **109**

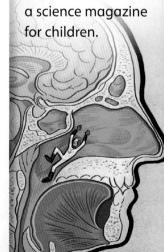

UNDERSTANDING VIRUSES
WITH MAX AXIOM SUPER SCIENTIST

Viruses may be small, but they can cause many kinds of diseases and illnesses in the human body. Today, super scientist Max Axiom hopes to get a better understanding of these fascinating, tiny visitors.

1

Viruses are much smaller than bacteria. They're so small that you can't see them with a regular microscope. You need a powerful electron microscope like this one to see them.

Here's a virus that causes the common cold.

2

Viruses cause many diseases in plants, animals, and people. I'll shrink down to their size to take a closer look.

I'll need to get smaller than cells ...

and bacteria ...

for a good view of viruses.

Think

What is the main idea of the reading so far?

3

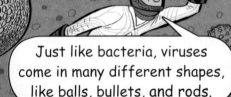

Just like bacteria, viruses come in many different shapes, like balls, bullets, and rods.

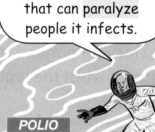

This is polio, a virus that can paralyze people it infects.

POLIO

INFLUENZA

Here's the influenza virus, which causes the flu.

At one time, people knew very little about viruses. Thanks to scientists like Max Axiom, humans can know much more about these viruses and how to stay healthy when they attack.

Think

What is the theme of the reading?

Comprehension

 Think Were the pictures in the story useful or interesting? Why or why not? How did the pictures help you understand the information better?

A Circle the main idea and theme for the Max Axiom story.

1 The main idea of the story is:
   a Scientists need electron microscopes to see viruses.
   b Viruses that go into your nose often get trapped there.
   c Viruses are dangerous, but the human body can fight them.
   d Polio is a very dangerous virus.

2 The theme of the story is:
   a The human body works hard to keep you healthy.
   b Viruses and bacteria come in many shapes and sizes.
   c White blood cells are very powerful.
   d Scientists know everything about the human body.

B Circle True (T) or False (F).

1 All bacteria look the same.   T   F
2 The top layer of your skin has dead cells.   T   F
3 Stomach acids can destroy viruses.   T   F
4 White blood cells can hurt us.   T   F
5 You can see viruses with just your eyes.   T   F
6 Mucus helps your body stay healthy.   T   F

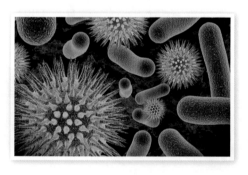

C **Words in Context** Match each clue to a word. Write the correct letter.

1 If a person did this, they ate food. _____   a suit

2 You can wear this on your body. _____   b scrape

3 This describes water, juice, oil, or blood. _____   c swallowed

4 If you have one of these, your skin may hurt. _____ d fluid

Grammar in Use

D Listen and sing along. **Get Back in Bed!** 🔊 2·32

It's a nice, warm, and sunny day.
I want to go outside and play.
"You cannot play. Get back in bed!
You're much too sick," my mother said.

She says I have the common cold.
My head aches, and I'm hot and cold.
I sneeze and blow. I blow and sneeze.
More soft, white paper tissues – please!

E Read the sentence. What do the three underlined words describe?

It's a <u>nice</u>, <u>warm</u>, and <u>sunny</u> day.

F **Learn Grammar** Order of Adjectives

You can use more than one adjective to describe a noun. The adjectives must go in a certain order: opinion … size … age … shape … color … kind.

Max Axiom studies these fascinating, tiny visitors.
opinion   size

Read each sentence. Write the adjectives in the correct order.

1 The doctor washed his white, new, lab coat. _____

2 Max saw round, red, large viruses. _____

3 It's a tiny, gray, ugly polio virus. _____

G Describe objects in your classroom using two or three adjectives. Make a list like the one below. Then describe the objects to your partner.

> There is a long, white, plastic ruler on my desk.

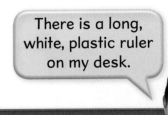

Things in my classroom
long, white, plastic ruler

Communicate

Listening

 Think Why do students in the same school often catch the same cold?

A Listen. Then match the two parts of each sentence. 🔊 2·33

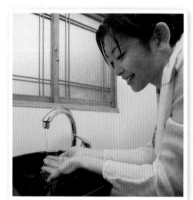

1 Wash your hands • • **a** with a tissue when you sneeze or cough.

2 Don't touch your eyes, nose, or mouth • • **b** often each day.

3 Cover your mouth and nose • • **c** by taking care of your body.

4 Stay healthy • • **d** with your fingers.

B Listen again. Write the correct answer. 🔊 2·34

1 How long should you wash your hands for? _____

2 Where can viruses get into your body? _____

3 What happens if you sneeze without a tissue? _____

4 How often should you exercise? _____

Speaking 🔊 2·35

C With your partner, ask and answer personal questions about sickness and health.

> What do you do when you catch a cold?

> I drink a lot of water and … What do you do?

> I usually …

> How do you stay healthy?

> I try to … What about you?

> I usually … and …

Word Study

D Learn Antonyms

Remember, **antonyms** are words that have opposite meanings.

The skin's top layer is made of **dead** cells, so viruses can't find **live** cells to infect.

Listen and read the words. Draw arrows to connect the antonyms below. Then write a sentence for each word in your notebook. 2·36

shrink dead inhale live expand exhale

A-Z

Writing Study

E Learn Give Advice with Commands

You can give **advice** to another person with a **command**. When you give advice with a command, you don't need to write the subject (the pronoun *you*).

Eat healthy food every day.
Don't touch your eyes with your fingers.

Read each sentence. Rewrite it as a simple command.

1 You should wash your hands every day. _____**Wash your hands every day.**_____

2 You need to protect yourself from viruses. _____

3 You shouldn't touch your mouth or nose. _____

4 You should buy tissues during the flu season. _____

5 You shouldn't forget to exercise often. _____

 Now practice writing in the **Workbook**. page 104

Vocabulary: Antonyms • Writing: Give Advice with Commands **Unit 11 115**

BIG QUESTION 6

?

How do our bodies work?

Our bodies protect us against viruses.

Good health habits help our bodies work well.

Words

A Listen and say the words. Then read and listen to the sentences. 🔊 2•37

system	blood	heart	arteries	veins	capillary

lungs	trachea	diaphragm	carbon dioxide	pulse

1 Each **system** in your body has many parts working together.

2 **Blood** carries oxygen throughout your body.

3 Jodi's **heart** beat quickly as she ran up the stairs.

4 Arthur eats low-fat food to keep his **arteries** healthy.

5 Sasha could see tiny blue **veins** under her skin.

6 A **capillary** is smaller than an artery or a vein.

7 Andy has powerful **lungs** because he exercises often.

8 Your **trachea** lets air into your lungs.

9 The baby's **diaphragm** moved in and out as she slept.

10 We breathe **carbon dioxide** out of our mouths.

11 Peter could feel his **pulse** in his wrist.

B Put the following words into the correct category. Talk about your choices.

arteries	diaphragm	heart	capillaries	veins	lungs	trachea

Helps People Breathe		Helps Move Blood	

C Circle True (T) or False (F).

1 A system is made up of many things. T F

2 Carbon dioxide is a liquid. T F

3 You have a pulse if you are alive. T F

4 Only people have blood. T F

Before You Read

 Think When you breathe, do you breathe through your nose or mouth? What part of your body moves in and out?

D **Learn** Sequence of Actions

Many nonfiction readings describe important actions that happen in a specific order, or **sequence**. Look for clue words to help you understand the sequence. These words include *first, next, then, as a result, while, during, before, after, last,* and *finally*.

Read the paragraph. Then number the actions below in the order in which they happen.

Before Sara goes jogging, she prepares her body for it. First, she stretches for five minutes. Next, she walks for one kilometer to get her legs warmed up and ready for her jog. Then she jogs for 30 minutes. After jogging, she slows down and walks again for two kilometers. Finally, she stops and stretches for another ten minutes.

_____ She walks for one kilometer.

_____ She stretches for ten minutes.

_____ She jogs for 30 minutes.

_____ She walks for two kilometers.

____1____ She stretches for five minutes.

E **Words in Context** Scan the reading on pages 118–119 and circle these words. As you read, guess what the words mean.

> **major   pumps   tubes   squeezes**

F Look at the illustration on the next page. What body parts do you see? What do you know about these body parts? What jobs do those parts do?

PREVIEW

The Human Body: Systems at Work

In this *informational text*, you will read about two major systems in the human body and how they work together for good health. Remember, informational texts give information about a specific topic. As you read, look for clue words to help you understand the sequence of the actions in the reading.

Life Science

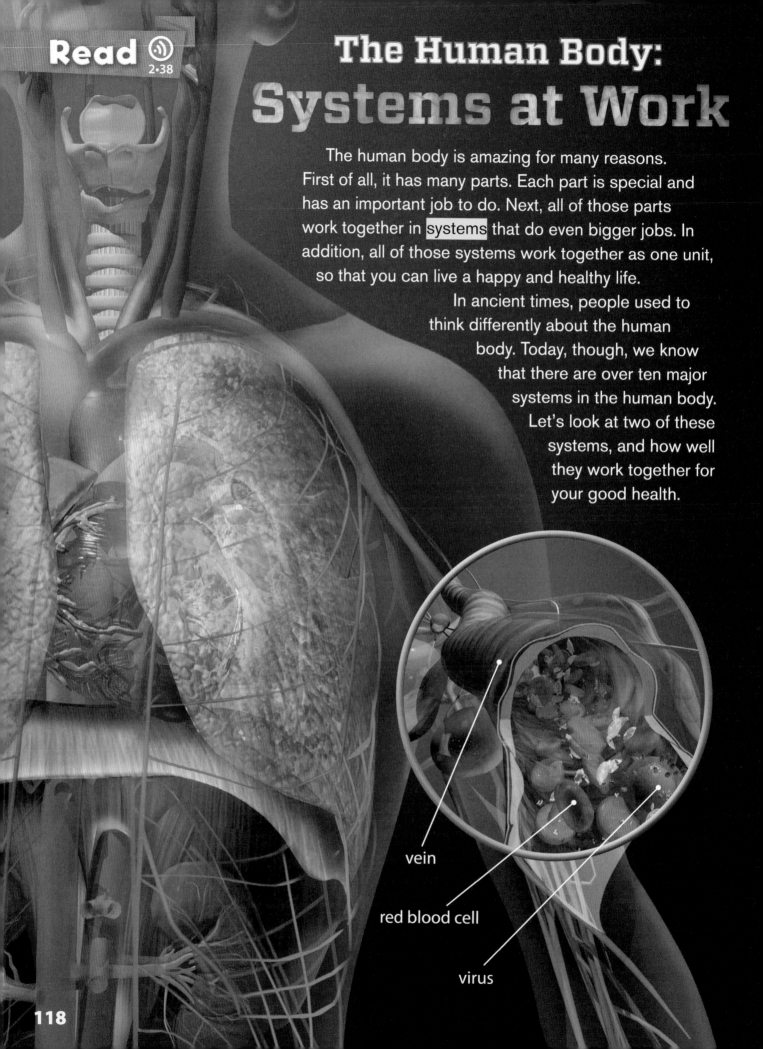

The Human Body: Systems at Work

The human body is amazing for many reasons. First of all, it has many parts. Each part is special and has an important job to do. Next, all of those parts work together in systems that do even bigger jobs. In addition, all of those systems work together as one unit, so that you can live a happy and healthy life.

In ancient times, people used to think differently about the human body. Today, though, we know that there are over ten major systems in the human body. Let's look at two of these systems, and how well they work together for your good health.

vein

red blood cell

virus

The Respiratory System

This system brings oxygen into your body and takes carbon dioxide out of your body. The major parts of the respiratory system are the trachea, the lungs, and the diaphragm.

The Circulatory System

This system carries oxygen and food to all of the cells in your body. It then removes carbon dioxide and other waste products from those cells. The major parts of the circulatory system are the heart, the arteries, the veins, the capillaries, and the blood that moves through those parts.

Two Systems Working Together as One

When you breathe in, your diaphragm first helps your lungs to get bigger. As a result, the air flows into your nose or mouth, through your trachea, and into your lungs. This air has oxygen, which your body needs to live. Next, the oxygen in your lungs passes into the capillaries, which then carry blood to the pulmonary vein. This vein then takes the blood to the left side of your heart.

Your heart pumps this blood into tubes called arteries, which then carry oxygen to all of the cells in your body. Next, these cells use this oxygen to keep your body healthy. They also create carbon dioxide after they use the oxygen. Your body doesn't need carbon dioxide, so your blood takes it away. After veins carry this blood back to the right side of your heart, it is pumped back into your lungs. The carbon dioxide then passes back into the air in your lungs. Finally, when your diaphragm squeezes your lungs, the air rushes out of your body.

These two systems work together to bring oxygen-rich blood to every part of your body within one minute. They do this 24 hours a day, while you sleep, eat, study, and play. It is easy to see why the human body is called the most amazing machine in the world.

Think

What is the sequence of actions up to now?

Think

What is the sequence of actions in this paragraph?

You **BREATHE** about **20,000 times** every day.

Check Your Lung Power!

1. Get a package of large balloons. Make sure they are all the same size. Give one to each friend.

2. Tell everyone to blow ONCE into their balloons, filling them as much as possible. Then measure the balloons. Whose is the biggest?

Put your **two fists together**. This is about the size of your **HEART**.

Check Your Heartbeat!

1. Place two fingers on your wrist below your thumb. Can you feel blood moving through the artery? This is your pulse, which measures your heartbeat.

2. Count the number of beats you feel in one minute. Compare your heartbeat with your friends.

Understand

Comprehension

 Think Tell your partner three interesting things you learned about the circulatory and respiratory systems.

A Number the steps in the correct order.

Part One

_____ The lungs put oxygen into the blood.

_____ Blood goes from the lungs to the heart.

__1__ Oxygen goes into the lungs from the trachea.

Part Two

_____ Blood goes back to the heart through the veins.

__4__ Blood goes from the heart into the arteries.

_____ Blood gives oxygen to cells and takes carbon dioxide.

Part Three

__7__ Blood goes from the heart to the lungs.

_____ Carbon dioxide goes out of the lungs through the trachea.

_____ The lungs take carbon dioxide out of blood.

B Answer the questions.

1 What two things does your diaphragm do?

2 What does the blood in your arteries carry?

3 Why do arteries go everywhere in your body?

4 What waste product do you breathe out?

C **Words in Context** Complete each sentence with a word from the box.

| major   pump   tube   squeeze |

1 A fire engine can _____ water through a fire hose.

2 Don't _____ the balloon, or it will pop!

3 The lungs are a _____ part of the respiratory system.

4 The science teacher filled the long _____ with water.

Grammar in Use

D **Listen and read along.** 🔊 2•39

When I was a baby, I used to ride my bike to Grandma's house.

You rode your bike to your grandmother's house?

Well, I had to. I didn't know how to walk yet.

E **Read the sentences. Which sentence shows what someone did often?**

a When I was young, I used to ride my bike.   **b** I rode my bike today.

F **Learn Grammar** *Used To*

Use **used to** before an action that happened often in the past, but not now.

In ancient times, people used to think differently about the human body.

XXXXX |
Past   Present   Future

Compare this to an action that happened one time in the past.

Last week, I thought about the circulatory system.

X |
Past   Present   Future

Circle the correct answer.

1 My sister **used to go** / **went** to the swimming pool often as a child.
2 Sandra **used to go** / **went** to the store yesterday.
3 My father **used to play** / **played** games with his friends many years ago.

G **Make a chart like the one below. Then talk to your partner about it.**

I used to take the bus to school. I took the subway to school on Friday.

Things I did often	Things I did one time
used to take the bus	took the subway

Communicate

Listening

 Think Why do our bodies need bones? How do bones help our bodies?

A Listen. Match each speaker to a fact. 🔊 2·40

1 Eduardo	2 Wendy	3 Kaya	4 Subin
●	●	●	●
●	●	●	●
a	**b**	**c**	**d**
Only one bone in the skull can move.	An adult has 206 bones.	Each hand has 27 bones.	The spine has 26 bones.

B Listen again. Circle True (T) or False (F). 🔊 2·41

1   Adult humans have more bones than babies do.   T   F

2   The bones in the spine are shaped like rings.   T   F

3   The skull is made up of one bone.   T   F

4   Your feet have more bones than your hands.   T   F

Speaking 🔊 2·42

C **Learn** Explanations with *That* or *Where*

When you need to explain what something is, use the words **that** or **where** to add more information.

What is the stomach?

It's a part of your body.
not much information

It's a part of your body **that** breaks down food.
more information

It's a part of your body **where** food goes.
more information

Explain what things are with your partner. Use *that* or *where*.

What is the heart?

It's the part of the body that …

What is … ?

It's … where …

Word Study

D Learn — Verbs that End in -ate

Nouns that end in -ation can often become verbs by changing the ending to -ate.

Good circulation **is very important for your body.** (noun)
This system circulates **your blood.** (verb)

Listen and read the words. Then complete the verbs in the chart. 2·43

navigate   duplicate   estimate   concentrate   exaggerate   graduate

Noun	Verb	Noun	Verb
1 estimation		4 exaggeration	
2 graduation		5 duplication	
3 navigation		6 concentration	

Writing Study

E Learn — Subject / Verb Agreement with Indefinite Pronouns

Many indefinite pronouns, such as *anyone*, *everyone*, *somebody*, *anything*, and *no one*, are followed by a singular verb in a sentence.

When everyone works **together, you can do great things!**
Anything is possible when you work hard.

Circle the correct verb.

1 Everyone **need** / **needs** to exercise to keep their bodies strong.

2 Something **is** / **are** in your blood that your cells need. What is it?

3 **Do** / **Does** anyone know what a capillary is?

4 Nobody **want** / **wants** to get hurt when they play a sport.

5 Everything in the science book **is** / **are** fascinating.

 Now practice writing in the Workbook. page 112

Wrap Up

Writing

A Read Max's interview with a part of the body.

Title —— **An Interview with the Human Heart**

Introduction —
Max: Good morning, Heart. How's it going today?
Heart: It's going great, Max. I'm working, as usual.

Questions —
Max: What do you do, Heart?

Answers —
Heart: I pump blood through the body.

Max: How often do you pump?

Heart: All the time. I pump about 70 times each minute.

Max: I see. Where are you located in the human body?

Heart: I'm in the chest area, a little to the left side, under the rib cage. That's a group of bones that protects me and the lungs.

Max: What do you look like inside?

Heart: I have four chambers. They are like rooms inside me.

Max: You have an important job to do.

Heart: Yes. I'm a very busy body part, and I never get a break!

Closing —
Max: Well, I'll let you get back to work. Thanks for talking to me today!
Heart: Of course, Max. Come back anytime. I'll be pumping with a smile!

B Answer the questions.

1 How many times does a human heart usually pump each minute?
2 What is inside a human heart?

Learn Interview

- Brainstorm interesting questions that you want answers to.
- Do research to find the correct answers to these questions.
- Write your interview as if you are really talking with someone.
- Include an introduction and a closing in your interview.

 Write Now go to the **Workbook** to plan and write your own interview. page 113 ⟩

Project: Conducting an Interview

C **Conduct an interview with a human body part. Then perform it.**

- In pairs, read your interviews to each other and talk about them.

- Choose which interview you want to perform for the class. Decide who will lead the interview and who will be the body part.

- Decide what to add to make the interview more interesting. You can add more information or props, such as simple costumes.

- Practice the interview with your partner a few times. Add actions or gestures to make the interview more interesting.

- Try to memorize most of your parts, and write down any words that you don't want to forget.

- Perform your interview for the class. Try to sound natural. Speak loudly and clearly.

Today I'm chatting with the skull. How's it going today?

It's going well, Olivia. I'm busy protecting the brain.

That's great! Are you made of just one bone?

Oh, no. I'm made of 22 bones.

BIG QUESTION 6

How do our bodies work?

A Watch the video.

B Think more about the Big Question. What did you learn?

C Complete the **Big Question Chart**.

What did you learn about the human body?

In units **13** and **14** you will:

WATCH a video about how people get information.

LEARN about different types of mass media.

READ an interview and a reporter's blog.

BIG QUESTION **7**

What is the mass media?

A Watch the video. ▶

B Look at the picture and talk about it.

1 What does each person have? What can they do with these things?

2 What do you think each person is looking at or reading about?

C Think and answer the questions.

1 Where do you get news and information?

2 What news did you hear today?

D Fill out the **Big Question Chart**.

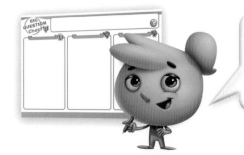

What do you know about the mass media? What do you want to know?

127

Words

A Listen and read the words. Listen again and say the words. 🔊 3·02

mass media

newspaper

magazine

printing press

publisher

advertising

broadcast

the Web

smartphone

blog

social network

B Circle the correct answer.

1	You can share your thoughts on this.	publisher	blog
2	Some people get this in the mail.	magazine	social network
3	You can check the news on this.	printing press	smartphone
4	Many people read this every day.	newspaper	broadcast
5	People use this to find information about anything.	advertising	the Web

C Answer the questions.

1 What forms of mass media do you use?

_____

2 Why do people use advertising?

_____

3 Why is a printing press helpful?

_____

Before You Read

 Think When do you learn new information about the world? How do you feel when you learn this new information?

D **Learn** Main Idea and Supporting Details

An entire reading will have one **main idea**. Also, each paragraph or section in the reading will usually have its own main idea. **Supporting details** explain the main idea of a reading or a paragraph.

Read the information. Write the main idea and three supporting details in the graphic organizer.

Derek is very interested in news from around the world. Every morning while he eats breakfast, he reads the newspaper. On the train to work, he uses his smartphone to check news on the Web. After he returns home at night, Derek watches news on television and then discusses it on a social network with his friends.

Main Idea _____

Supporting Detail	Supporting Detail	Supporting Detail
_____	_____	_____
_____	_____	_____
_____	_____	_____

E **Words in Context** Scan the reading on pages 130–131 and circle these words. As you read, guess what the words mean.

> **journalist**   **newsreels**   **radio station**   **latest**

F What news did you share with your friends today at school? Where did you hear this news?

From Newspapers to Smartphones: The Rise of the Mass Media

In this *interview*, an expert explains how the mass media began and how it continues to change as it brings news and information to people. In an interview, a person shares his or her knowledge on a subject. As you read, notice the main ideas in the reading and their supporting details.

Social Studies: Technology

From Newspapers to Smartphones:

Thanks to the mass media, news travels fast. Journalist Megan Michaels interviews Dr. Philip Kendall, a mass media expert.

Megan: Thank you for meeting with me, Dr. Kendall.

Dr. Kendall: You're welcome.

Megan: People like to share news, don't they?

Dr. Kendall: Absolutely. Long ago, when early humans discovered how to make fire, they told their friends. Then those friends told others. Ideas spread from person to person, and in fact, they still do. However, mass media is different. It brings news and knowledge to many people very quickly.

Megan: When did mass media begin?

Dr. Kendall: It began around 1440, when Johannes Gutenberg changed the way news traveled. You see, he invented the printing press. Before the printing press, people had to make copies of books by hand. Suddenly, this invention could make copies of books much more easily. Then, about 150 years later, people printed the first newspapers in Europe. Today, people around the world read newspapers every day.

Megan: How many newspapers are there?

Dr. Kendall: Newspapers, along with magazines, are very popular. There are over 6,000 daily newspapers in the world today. Publishers print almost 400 million copies each day. Magazines are popular because they focus on one subject, such as news, movies, fashion, or sports. Advertising helps to pay for the cost of publishing newspapers and magazines.

Megan: So what happened next in the history of mass media?

Dr. Kendall: Movies were the next form of mass media. People started going to movie theaters about 100 years ago.

Think

What is the main idea in this paragraph? What details support it?

1440s

1800s

1900s

1920s

The Rise of the Mass Media

These new "moving pictures" amazed people. Often, movie theaters showed newsreels, too. These were short films with news from around the world. People watched the news for the first time this way.

Megan: And then the television came next, right?

Think

What is the main idea in this paragraph? What details support it?

Dr. Kendall: Actually, the radio came next. It appeared about the same time as movies, but the first radio station didn't get started until about 1920. Today, there are over 44,000 radio stations around the world.

Megan: Do people still get their news from the radio?

Dr. Kendall: Yes, they do. Many radio stations report the news every hour. Some stations broadcast the news all the time. People can listen to the news while they drive or work.

Megan: When did the television appear?

Dr. Kendall: Television broadcasting started in the 1930s. Now, television is everywhere, bringing news and entertainment to people around the world. Some stations now offer 24-hour news. Events are broadcast live, while they are happening.

Megan: So people have a lot of choices for their news, don't they?

Dr. Kendall: They do, but you mustn't forget the latest choice—the Web! Today, almost one third of the people in the world use the Web, and this number will continue to grow. The Web, or Internet, lets us read news, watch videos, and share information through social networks and blogs. Many people think that the Web is now the most important form of mass media. Also, smartphones give us Web service, so you don't have to carry a computer to check the news.

Megan: We live in very interesting times.

Dr. Kendall: That's true. It will be exciting to see what's next in the world of mass media.

Think

What is the main idea of the entire interview? What details support it?

1930s

1950s

1980s

2000s

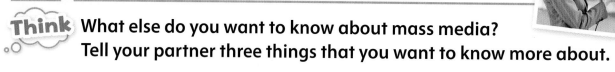

Understand

Comprehension

Think What else do you want to know about mass media?
Tell your partner three things that you want to know more about.

A Write the number for each detail beside the correct main idea in the chart.

1 One third of the people in the world use the Web.
2 There are over 6,000 daily newspapers in the world today.
3 These new "moving pictures" amazed people.
4 He invented the printing press around 1440.

Main Ideas	Detail
Gutenberg changed the way news traveled.	
Newspapers and magazines are very popular.	
Movies were new 100 years ago.	
The Web is used a lot today.	1

B Write the types of mass media in the order in which they appeared in history.

the Web   movies   television   radio   ~~newspapers~~

Oldest ⟶ **Newest**

newspapers   _____   _____   _____   _____

C **Words in Context** Read each numbered sentence. Then circle two correct answers for each sentence.

1 Megan Michaels is a <u>journalist</u>.
   a She writes music.   b She asks questions.   c She writes down information.

2 People watched <u>newsreels</u>.
   a Newsreels gave news.   b People saw them at theaters.   c They were long.

3 There are many <u>radio stations</u> in the world.
   a They broadcast news.   b They are not popular.   c Some broadcast music.

4 The Web is the <u>latest</u> choice for news.
   a It is an old choice.   b It is the newest choice.   c It didn't exist many years ago.

Grammar in Use

D Listen and sing along. **The News Today** 🔊 3·04

I have to know what happened.
I mustn't miss the news.
I must buy a newspaper,
But which one shall I choose?

You don't have to buy a paper.
You can use my new smartphone,
And we can check the Internet
While we're walking home.

E Read the sentences. Which one is about what someone needs to do?

a I must buy a newspaper.   **b** You don't have to buy a paper.

F **Learn Grammar** *Must, Mustn't, Have To, Don't Have To*

Use **must** and **have to** to talk about what a person needs to do.
Use **mustn't** to talk about what a person shouldn't do.
Use **don't have to** to talk about what a person doesn't need to do.

You **must** pay for the Internet to use it at home.
You **mustn't** take a newspaper without paying for it.
You **don't have to** carry a computer to check the news.

Read the sentences. Circle the correct verb.

1 Maki **has to** / **doesn't have to** help her mother cook because she has to study.

2 You **must** / **mustn't** bring your smartphone into class. Leave it in your locker.

3 Our teacher is not happy. He says we **have to** / **don't have to** study harder.

G Imagine you are a teacher. Make a chart like the one below. Then talk about it with your partner.

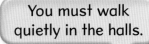

You must walk quietly in the halls.

Students must ...	Students mustn't ...
walk quietly	

Grammar: Must, Mustn't, Have To, Don't Have To   **Unit 13**   **133**

Communicate

Listening

 Think If you had a blog, what would you write about? When would you write it? Who would you want to read your blog?

A Listen. What is the girl talking about? Check (✓) the correct box. 🔊 3·05

☐ She's talking about how to find interesting blogs to read.

☐ She's talking about how to create and use a blog.

☐ She's talking about how to find photos and videos on the Web.

B Listen again. Answer the questions. 🔊 3·06

1 What kind of site does Tina use for her blog? _____

2 What does Tina write about? _____

3 When does Tina write on her blog? _____

4 What kind of mistakes does Tina check for? _____

5 What is Tina's only contact on the blog? _____

Speaking 🔊 3·07

C How do people you know get news? Share your ideas with your partner and give examples.

Word Study

D | **Learn** | Words with *Silent k*

Some words have letters that are silent. In words that begin with *kn-*, the **k** is silent.

Mass media brings knowledge to many people.

Listen and read the words. Then listen to the sentences. Write each *silent k* word you hear in your notebook. 3·08

> knowledge   knot   knight   knit   kneel   knuckle
>
> **A-Z**

Writing Study

E | **Learn** | Pronouns

Remember, **pronouns** are words that take the place of a noun or another pronoun. Pronouns should always agree with the words they take the place of.

When early humans discovered how to make fire, they told their friends.

They and *their* are pronouns for the noun *humans*.

Read the sentences. Circle the pronouns. Then draw arrows to the nouns they take the place of.

1   My grandfather reads the newspaper. Then (he) recycles (it).

2   The Internet gives people facts, but it also gives them opinions.

3   Jenny plays the radio when she does her homework.

4   Blogs are very useful. They help people share their thoughts.

 Write Now practice writing in the **Workbook.** page 123

BIG QUESTION 7

What is the mass media?

The mass media spreads facts and knowledge.

The mass media sends information to many people quickly.

UNIT 14 Get Ready

Words

A Listen and say the words. Then read and listen to the sentences. 🔊 3·09

| reporter | editor | interview | headline | hero | website |

| mistake | decide | discuss | investigate | search |

1 The **reporter** won an award for his newspaper article.

2 The **editor** made changes to the reporter's article.

3 She had an **interview** with the mayor.

4 The **headline** on the newspaper was about the fire.

5 Jim was a **hero** after he saved the child from the fire.

6 This news **website** has a lot of information.

7 Editors always check for **mistakes** in an article.

8 The editor **decides** which articles to put in the magazine.

9 Students will **discuss** what they learned from the blog.

10 The police will **investigate** the fire to see how it started.

11 Eric **searched** the newspaper for interesting stories.

B Two of the three words are correct. Cross out the wrong answer.

1 This person often works for a newspaper.

    editor   hero   reporter

2 A reporter may do this.

    website   investigate   search

3 You can read this.

    headline   website   hero

4 There must be two people to do this.

    discuss   interview   decide

C Answer these questions. Then discuss the answers with your partner.

1 When was the last time you made a mistake?

2 What kinds of websites do you search for?

Before You Read

Think What are some brave things that people do? How can you be brave?

D **Learn** Conflict and Resolution

An interesting story has a **conflict** (a problem that a character needs to solve) and a **resolution** (a solution to a problem). Usually, there are many *possible* resolutions in a story but only one *final* resolution.

Read the short story. Fill in the chart below.

The news photographer looked through his camera, but everything was black. He checked the battery, and it had full power. Then he made sure the power button was "on." He didn't know what to do! Suddenly, his friend said, "Hey, your lens cap is still on the camera." The photographer laughed, took off the lens cap, and took a picture of his friend.

Conflict	Possible Resolutions	Final Resolution
	check the battery's power	

E **Words in Context** Scan the story on pages 138–139 and circle these words. As you read, guess what they mean.

mansion   terrible   donated   fair

F Why are reporters an important part of the mass media? What does a reporter have to do to get information to use in a story?

From the Blog of
Elsa B. Garcia, Kid Reporter

In this *realistic fiction* story, a young reporter helps someone in need. Realistic fiction has characters, problems, and settings that seem real. As you read, think about the story's conflict and possible resolutions.

Elizabeth Cody Kimmel is the author of over 30 children's books. She lives near New York City.

From the Blog of
Elsa B. Garcia, Kid Reporter

July 5. I have decided to keep a blog so the world can read about all the things I investigate. Today I heard that they are going to tear down the old stone house across the street. The newspaper says the city government owns the house, and just one person lives there. Why does the city government own an old house? Who lives there? I have decided to find out because I want to save the house.

Think
What is the main conflict in the story?

July 6. I used the Internet to search for articles about old houses on my street. I found an entire website called *The Lost History of Stone House*. It said the stone building was once the gatehouse of a huge mansion. A family called the Martins lived there until one night a terrible fire burned the mansion down. The young daughter of a maid smelled the smoke and woke up every single person in the house. Everyone got out safely that night. The website showed the front page of an old newspaper with a story about the fire. The headline said: "Young Girl, 9, Saves Seven People in Mysterious Fire." She was the same age as me!

SUNDAY NEWS
Young Girl, 9, Saves Seven People in Mysterious Fire

July 7. I am going to visit the house to see if I can talk to the person who lives there. I have never done an interview before, and I'm very nervous. What if I make a mistake?

July 7, Part 2. I did it! A woman who looks like my grandmother answered the door. She said her name was Miss Lu, and that she would be happy to answer my questions. She knew all about the mansion and the fire. I learned that the Martin family donated a lot of money to the city to help build the library and the hospital. After the fire, they decided to move away and let the city have their land. I asked Miss Lu if she knew the Martins. She smiled and said no one had ever asked her that before. When she told me the answer, I couldn't believe it. My mom says I have to go to sleep now, so read my blog tomorrow for the rest of the story!

Miss Lu July 7th

Think

What possible resolutions are there to the conflict?

July 8. I'm back! Miss Lu knew the Martins because she lived in the mansion, too. Yes, readers, Miss Lu was the little girl who saved the family that night! I am writing a letter to the editor of our newspaper asking the mayor not to destroy the house. Miss Lu is a hero, and it isn't fair to take away her home!

July 10. Today, a television reporter came to interview me. You can watch it on Channel 7 tonight!

July 11. I have more wonderful news. My story will be on a radio show that will be broadcast to the entire city tonight!

July 15. Today I got an e-mail from the mayor. He said there will be a special meeting to discuss the house. I'm amazed that he took the time to write to me!

August 1. Awesome news! The mayor decided not to tear down the old house! He agrees that Miss Lu is a hero and should be able to live there as long as she likes. This is the first news story I have ever investigated. I love being a reporter, and I can't wait to find more stories!

Think

What is Elsa's final resolution to the conflict?

Understand

Comprehension

 Think What did the story teach you about the mass media?
Tell your partner two things you learned.

A Complete the chart about "From the Blog of Elsa B. Garcia, Kid Reporter."

Conflict	Possible Resolutions	Final Resolution
The city government will tear down the old stone house.		

B Answer the questions.

1 Why did Elsa decide to keep a blog?
2 Why is Miss Lu a hero?
3 How did Elsa help Miss Lu?

C **Words in Context** Match each sentence to a clue. Then match each clue to a conclusion.

1 The Martins lived in a huge <u>mansion</u>.

   a Libraries need money.

   e The underlined word means *a large house.*

2 The fire was <u>terrible</u>.

   b Taking away someone's home is bad.

   f The underlined word means *very bad.*

3 The Martins <u>donated</u> money to build the library.

   c The Martins had a big house.

   g The underlined word means *right* or *correct.*

4 It's not <u>fair</u> to take Miss Lu's home.

   d This fire burned down the house.

   h The underlined word means *gave away.*

Grammar
pages 128–129

Grammar in Use

D Listen and read along. 🔊 3·11

Harry doesn't read news magazines.

Really? I saw him buy one here this morning.

Oh, he has bought a news magazine many times.

That's because it's cheaper than sunglasses.

E Look at **D**. What has Harry done in the past?

F **Learn Grammar** Present Perfect

Use the **present perfect** tense to tell what happened in the past but did not happen at a specific time. Use the **past participle** form of the main verb with *has* or *have*.

I have decided to keep a blog.
past participle

He hasn't written a blog before.
past participle

Read the sentences. Underline the present perfect tense.

1 The reporter has done many interviews.

2 She hasn't met the newspaper editor.

3 Smartphones have changed the news business.

I haven't met a reporter before.

G Make a list like the one below. Then talk to your partner about it.

Things I haven't done
meet a reporter

Communicate

Listening

 Think When are facts important in the news? When are opinions important in the news?

A Listen. Decide if each piece of news below is a fact or an opinion. Circle the correct answer. 🔊 3·12

News	Fact or Opinion?
1 The cooks will serve spaghetti with tomato sauce.	F O
2 The Westview soccer team did their very best.	F O
3 No one likes a rainy day.	F O
4 The sports festival is from 10:00 to 4:00 on Saturday.	F O

B Listen again. Answer the questions. 🔊 3·13

1 What was the score of the soccer game? _____

2 What should students bring because of the rain? _____

3 When is the school sports festival? _____

Speaking 🔊 3·14

C **Learn** Giving Opinions

Give your opinion using **I think** or **I don't think**. Use **because** to add a reason.

I think that nature blogs are interesting. **I don't think** that all blogs are interesting because some are boring.

Share your opinions about the mass media with your partner. Give reasons for your opinions.

> I think reporters have a difficult job.

> Why do you think that?

> I think that because …

> Yes, that's true. I think that … because …

Word Study

D **Learn** Synonyms

Remember, **synonyms** are words that have similar meanings.

One night, a terrible fire burned the mansion down.
One night, an awful fire burned the mansion down.

Listen and read the words. Then match the sentences with synonyms. 3·15

entire	huge	immense	special	unusual	whole

A-Z

1 It broadcasts to the *entire* city.   ●   ● **a** It's an *immense* home.

2 The mayor has a *special* meeting.   ●   ● **b** The *whole* city can listen.

3 The family lived in a *huge* mansion. ●   ● **c** The meeting is *unusual*.

Writing Study

E **Learn** Regular and Irregular Verbs in the Present Perfect

Remember, use the present perfect to tell what happened in the past. Use *has* or *have* with the **past participle** of a main verb. For regular main verbs, add **-ed**.

George has learned a lot from this science blog.

For irregular main verbs, the past participle has different forms.

I've seen the inside of a television studio.

Read each sentence. Write the past participle form of the verb in parentheses.

        written
1 William has (~~write~~) six books, and all of them are bestsellers.

2 The reporter has (investigate) many unusual events.

3 Lily has (go) to South America to report on the news there.

4 Marco has (build) his own radio from a kit.

 Write Now practice writing in the **Workbook.** page 131

Wrap Up

Writing

A Read this news story about a real event.

Headline — **New Water Park Opens in Elmwood**

Byline — by Elena Whitehall

Lead — The Elmwood Water Park has opened just in time for summer. The 20-acre park has something for everyone.

Facts and Quotations — Young children will love the splash pool, where they can run through spraying water. Older children will enjoy the five exciting waterslides. One of the slides drops 10 meters for those who like thrills. Serious swimmers will enjoy the new 25-meter lap pool. "I've never been in such a nice swimming pool," said one visitor.

Mayor Julie Swanson is very happy about the new park. "I'm very proud of this addition to Elmwood," she said. "This new park will bring friends and families together throughout the summer months."

The park is open 7 days a week, from 10:00 a.m. to 5:00 p.m. It's free and open to the public. Children under 12 must have a parent with them. The park is on the west side of the city, across from the zoo.

B Answer the questions.

1 What features of the park will people like?

2 Who can go to the park without their parents?

3 How many hours per day is the park open?

Learn · News Story

- A news story answers *who*, *what*, *when*, *where*, and *why*.

- It has a headline (title) and a byline (writer's name).

- It has a lead (introduction paragraph) that catches the reader's attention.

- Often, it includes information and quotations from an interview.

- All the information in a news story should be true and correct.

 Write Now go to the **Workbook** to plan and write your own news story. page 132

Project: Creating a School News Program

C **Create and perform a school news program.**

- In your group, discuss recent school events. Each person will report on one recent event in a news program.

- Decide what each person will report on, such as school lunches, sports, art news, or weather.

- Decide how to make your news program interesting, and choose the order of speakers.

- Practice your news program with your group. Speak slowly and clearly.

- Try to memorize what you will say, but write down important words and phrases if you need to.

- Perform your news program for the class. Pretend you are on television while you perform your news program.

> There is big news today! The library has decided that students can check out six books instead of four.

> In art news, Eva Martinez has won a special award in the city's art contest.

> Today's temperature will be 32 degrees Celsius. Drink lots of water.

BIG QUESTION 7

What is the mass media?

A **Watch the video.**

B **Think more about the Big Question. What did you learn?**

C **Complete the Big Question Chart.**

> What did you learn about the mass media?

In units **15** and **16** you will:

WATCH
a video about nature's power.

LEARN
about forces of nature.

READ
about natural forces and a family that faces one.

WRITE
a how-to
speech.

CREATE
an emergency
poster.

BIG QUESTION ⑧

What can we learn from nature's power?

A Watch the video. ▶

B Look at the picture and talk about it.

1 What do you see? How does it make you feel?

2 If you were in this place, what would you do?

C Think and answer the questions.

1 What types of bad weather or natural forces do you have in your area?

2 What can you do to prepare for bad weather or natural forces?

D Fill out the **Big Question Chart**.

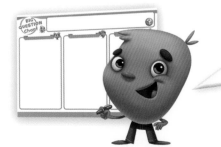

What do you know about nature's power? What do you want to know?

147

Get Ready

Words

A Listen and read the words. Listen again and say the words. 🔊 3·16

 flood

 earthquake

 tsunami

 hurricane

 tornado

 blizzard

 thunderstorm

 rescue worker

 victim

 power lines

 collapse

B Circle True (T) or False (F).

1	A tornado is like a dangerous moving column.	T	F
2	A blizzard can happen without snow.	T	F
3	An earthquake can't crack streets and move buildings.	T	F
4	Rescue workers must be brave and helpful.	T	F
5	A victim helps other people.	T	F
6	Heavy rain doesn't cause floods.	T	F
7	Hurricanes are large and shaped like a circle.	T	F
8	A tsunami isn't dangerous to people on a coast.	T	F

C Complete the sentences with the following words.

> thunderstorm   collapsed   power lines

Strong winds made the _____ shake up and down during

the _____ . Some of them even _____ .

Before You Read

 Think Do you think it is important to understand natural forces? Why or why not?

D **Learn** Cause and Effect in a Series of Events

Remember, a **cause** happens first. An **effect** happens next because of the cause. Cause and effect can also describe a series of events. A cause can create more than one effect.

Cause	First Effect	Second Effect
Snow fell through the night.	Schools closed the next day.	All the students were happy.

Read the sentences. What is the cause? What effects happen because of it?

 Yesterday, it rained very hard, and the river rose too high. Grace and her family climbed to the roof of their house. Rescue workers came in a boat. They took the family to safety.

Cause: **It rained very hard.**

1ˢᵗ Effect: _____

2ⁿᵈ Effect: _____

3ʳᵈ Effect: _____

4ᵗʰ Effect: _____

E **Words in Context** Scan the reading on pages 150–151 and circle these words. As you read, guess what the words mean.

> forces   funnel   horizontally   vertically

F Quickly look at the pictures in the article on the following two pages. How do you feel when you look at them? How are they alike and different?

Forces of Nature

In this *science article,* you will read about forces of nature that can cause harm to living things. Science articles are often full of scientific facts and powerful photographs. As you read about each force of nature, think about its cause and the effects of the cause.

Earth Science

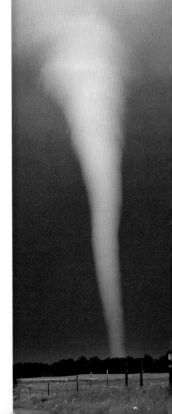

FORCES OF NATURE

Earth is a beautiful planet. Its oceans and lakes, blue skies, and rich land give us what we need to live. However, nature also has a very powerful side. It creates forces that can cause great harm to human life and property.

EARTHQUAKES

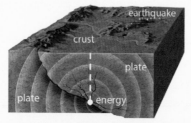

The outside part of Earth is the crust. Under the crust are many pieces called plates. The plates create energy when they move against each other. In an earthquake, the plates release this energy quickly. This energy moves the ground. In strong earthquakes, objects and even buildings can collapse.

When an earthquake happens under the ocean, parts of the ocean floor may rise or fall suddenly. This can create a tsunami. A tsunami travels very fast through the water. When it reaches a coast, it pushes huge amounts of water onto the land.

This water can destroy everything in its path. In 2011, many people died on the coast of eastern Japan in a large tsunami. Many rescue workers helped the victims of this disaster.

HURRICANES

A hurricane is a large, violent storm. It forms over warm ocean water and can grow to over 500 kilometers wide. Hurricane winds can blow from 100 to 250 kilometers per hour. When a large hurricane reaches land, it can destroy buildings and homes. The ocean water can rise and create floods. A large hurricane can knock down many trees and hurt plants, fish, and coral along a coast.

Think

What is the cause of an earthquake? What effects happen after it?

150

TORNADOES

Have you ever seen a real tornado? A tornado often looks like a funnel, and has strong spinning winds of up to 400 kilometers per hour. These winds can easily destroy homes and trees. An average tornado is about 75 meters wide near the ground, but some can be much larger. Tornadoes often form before a thunderstorm, when warm air in the atmosphere starts to spin horizontally across the sky and then vertically toward the ground. North America has more tornadoes than any other place in the world.

thunderstorm

tornado

warm, humid air

cool, dry air

Think

What is the cause of a tornado? What effects happen after it?

BLIZZARDS

In cold climates, snowy days are common. However, sometimes blizzards completely cover an area. Blizzards are very dangerous to drive in, because drivers can't see far away and may lose control of their cars on the snowy roads. Heavy snow can also break power lines and the roofs of homes. People who are outside in a blizzard can get lost, and the cold, windy air can freeze skin that isn't covered up. Blizzards can go on for days, which is dangerous for people who run out of food or need medical care.

Luckily, there are warning systems for these natural disasters. People in some countries can receive a message on their cell phones seconds before an earthquake strikes. Tsunami warning systems can give people time to leave the coast and move to a safe place. Modern weather systems warn people about weather conditions that may create tornadoes and blizzards. All of these systems help us prepare for nature's power.

snow

cold air

snow

Snow falls into warm air and melts into rain.

rain

warm air

cold air

Snow falls into cold air and never melts on the way down.

blizzard

Understand

Comprehension

 Think Which force of nature is the most interesting? Tell your partner your ideas.

A Connect each force of nature to a cause and two effects.

Force of Nature	First Effect	Second Effect
1 Earthquake: Earth's plates suddenly release energy.	**a** The storm grows and reaches land.	**e** Buildings and objects shake.
2 Hurricane: Warm ocean air forms a storm.	**b** This spinning air reaches the ground.	**f** Drivers can't see and are not safe.
3 Tornado: Warm air starts to spin.	**c** Snow covers the roads.	**g** Trees fall and floods happen.
4 Blizzard: Heavy snow falls. Strong winds blow.	**d** This energy moves the ground.	**h** It destroys everything in its path.

B Answer the questions.

1 Why is a tsunami so dangerous?
2 Which has stronger winds, a hurricane or a tornado?
3 What kinds of warnings can people receive?

C **Words in Context** Complete the sentences with the words in the box.

1 The weather balloon rose _____ into the air.

2 The dark _____ of the tornado looked scary.

3 Snow blew _____ across the road.

4 An earthquake's _____ can crack a street.

force
funnel
vertically
horizontally

Grammar in Use

D Listen and sing along. **Nature's Power**  3·18

> Have you ever felt an earthquake?
> No! Thank goodness.
> I've never felt an earthquake,
> And I hope I never do!
>
> Have you ever seen a tornado?
> Yes! One time!
> I once saw a tornado,
> But it was on TV!

E Look at **D**. Has Meg ever experienced an earthquake?

F **Learn Grammar** Present Perfect with *Ever* and *Never*

Use the present perfect with **ever** and **never** to ask and answer questions about life experiences.

Have you ever seen a real tornado?

Yes, I have. / No, I haven't. I've never seen a real tornado.

Add the word *ever* to each question. Then answer the question.

1 Have you experienced an earthquake?

<u>**Have you ever experienced an earthquake? Yes, I have.**</u>

2 Have you escaped from a hurricane?

_____

3 Has your teacher driven in a blizzard?

_____

G Make a chart about experiences. Ask your partner about them.

> Have you ever watched a scary movie?

Experience	Response
watched a scary movie	yes

Communicate

Listening

 Think Why is it important to stay calm during a natural disaster?

A Listen. Match each problem to a solution. 3·19

Problem		Solution

1 Large objects can fall down in your home during an earthquake. ● | ● **a** Decide on a safe place before an earthquake happens.

2 You don't know where to go in your home if an earthquake happens. ● | ● **b** Keep extra supplies in a safe room in your home.

3 There may be no electricity or running water if an earthquake happens. ● | ● **c** Attach large pieces of furniture to the wall.

B Listen again. Circle True (T) or False (F). 3·20

When an earthquake happens …

1 It's important to be prepared. **T F**

2 If you are outdoors, climb a tree. **T F**

3 Use a radio or smartphone to get information. **T F**

Speaking 3·21

C **Learn** Possibilities

When you aren't sure about the future, use the words **might**, **may**, and **could**.

What will the weather be like today?
There might be a lot of rain.
There could even be a tornado.
It may come close to our city.

Talk about possibilities with your partner.

What will the concert be like?

It might be …

What will … be like?

I think it could …

Word Study

D | **Learn** | Compound Nouns with Noun-Verb Combinations

Some **compound nouns** are made from a noun and a verb. When we say these compound nouns, the stress is usually on the first word.

In an earthquake, the plates release energy quickly.
      noun verb

Listen and read the words. Underline the two parts of each compound noun. 3·22

| snowfall | haircut | teamwork | raindrop | landslide | bodyguard |

A-Z

Writing Study

E | **Learn** | Contractions in Present Perfect Sentences

You can use **contractions** in present perfect sentences with subject pronouns.

We've bought extra water in case of a storm. (we + have = we've)
She's seen a tornado in her town. (she + has = she's)

Read the paragraph. Make contractions with the subject pronouns.

Teresa has experienced many forces of nature in her life in Mexico.
She's
~~She has~~ experienced a small earthquake that was quite scary. She has

also been in a hurricane. I have only been in a blizzard. My family

hasn't been in many dangerous situations. We have usually been safe!

 Write Now practice writing in the **Workbook.** page 142

BIG QUESTION 8

? **What can we learn from nature's power?**

Nature can be dangerous.

Warning systems are important for people's safety.

Words

A Listen and say the words. Then read and listen to the sentences. 🔊 3·23

| emergency | storm shelter | first-aid kit | cash | storm shutters | sleeping bag |

| flashlight | batteries | supplies | bottled water | canned food |

1 Fire fighters are always ready for an **emergency**.

2 The family stayed in the **storm shelter** during the tornado.

3 Billy's mother used her **first-aid kit** when Billy cut his finger.

4 Minju didn't have any **cash** to buy a sandwich.

5 Many houses near the ocean have **storm shutters**.

6 Take a **sleeping bag** on the overnight camping trip.

7 A **flashlight** is useful if there is no electricity.

8 Small radios and flashlights often need **batteries** to work.

9 You can buy emergency **supplies** at a supermarket.

10 The campers took **bottled water** on their trip.

11 Be sure to pack a can opener with the **canned food**.

B Two of the three words are correct. Cross out the wrong answer.

1 This helps you get what you need.
   supplies   storm shutters   cash

2 This can help you see in the dark.
   sleeping bag   flashlight   battery

3 This can help you if you are hurt or in danger.
   storm shelter   first-aid kit   emergency

4 This can help you if you are thirsty or hungry.
   flashlight   bottled water   canned food

5 This can protect you from cold winds.
   storm shutters   canned food   sleeping bag

C Use the word *emergency* in a sentence.

Before You Read

Think Were you ever in an emergency? If so, what was it like?

D Learn Making Inferences

Remember, as you read you can make a strong guess about something if you have enough information. This guess is called an **inference**. Use information from the reading plus your own knowledge to make inferences.

Reading Text	The clouds turn very dark.
My Knowledge	Dark clouds often bring rain.
My Inference	It's going to rain.

Read each paragraph. Then circle the correct inference.

1

Emma looked out of her living room window. The sky was getting very dark. Suddenly, Emma heard a voice from the television. "This is an emergency," the voice said. "Go to your basement or a room in the center of your house. Stay away from windows."

   a A dangerous storm was coming.
   b All houses have basements.

2

As David studied at the dining room table, the room started to shake gently. He stopped studying and waited, but the shaking became stronger. He quickly got under the table.

   a David was tired of studying.
   b David felt an earthquake.

E Words in Context Scan the story on pages 158–159 and circle these words. As you read, guess what the words mean.

> inland   destroyed   trunk   landfall

F Why is it important to stay calm during an emergency?

Staying Calm Before the Storm

In this *historical fiction* story, Luis and his family prepare to get away from a hurricane. Historical fiction tells a story from the past and often has a real setting, but the characters are usually not real. As you read, make inferences about the characters and events in the story.

Staying Calm Before the Storm

The state of Quintana Roo in Mexico's Yucatán Peninsula has experienced many hurricanes. Luis Sandoval lived in the capital city of Chetumal when Hurricane Dean hit the coast. He was nine years old.

On August 17, 2007, Luis Sandoval was eating a sandwich after school when the phone rang. It was his father, who worked for the city government in Chetumal.

"Luis, is your mother there?" he asked.

"No, Papa. She went to the supermarket with Pablo and Alex."

"Please listen carefully. Hurricane Dean is moving in our direction. It will reach our coast in three or four days. The government has declared a state of emergency."

Luis's heart started to beat quickly. "Are we in danger, Papa?"

"Not if we prepare. It may be as bad as Hurricane Wilma. Do you remember what we did then?"

"Yes, Papa."

"Then start preparing. All of you need to leave Chetumal and go further inland tomorrow morning. I will have to stay here."

His father hung up.

Luis remembered Hurricane Wilma very well. A rise in the ocean, called a storm surge, flooded large areas along the coast. Almost 600 millimeters of rain fell in many places. Waves as high as eight meters smashed violently into the third floors of hotels. Winds up to 240 kilometers per hour destroyed homes.

Now the state of Quintana Roo was prepared for Hurricane Dean. The government was ready to help people leave the area. For those who couldn't leave, there were 530 local storm shelters with food, blankets, and medicine. However, families also had to protect themselves. Luis checked the emergency list in the storage room and gathered the following items:

Think

Make an inference. How does Luis feel when he hears about the emergency?

EMERGENCY LIST
20 liters of bottled water
1 large box of dry and canned food
1 small radio with batteries
1 first-aid kit
2 flashlights
3 boxes of tissue paper
4 sleeping bags
emergency cash

Luis took out two small backpacks for his little brothers. They contained some clothes and were easy to carry. He took out two large backpacks for his mother and himself. He put some of the food, water, and supplies in each one. The rest of the supplies would go in the trunk of the car.

Suddenly, Luis's mother appeared in the doorway. His little brothers, Pablo and Alex, were holding her hands tightly.

"Your father called me," his mother said. "I tried to buy food and water, but they turned us away at the supermarket. There were too many people there."

"Don't worry, Mama," said Luis. "I've already packed everything we need."

"Good," said his mother. "We have storm shutters, but you and I have to help Aunt Alma put boards over her windows tonight. We'll leave early tomorrow morning."

The next morning, Luis, his mother, his aunt, and his brothers left the city. They drove many kilometers inland and stayed at a storm shelter. They would be safe from the hurricane there. Luis's father remained in Chetumal, helping those who could not leave the city.

Think

Make an inference. How is Luis different from his younger brothers?

Hurricane Dean made landfall near the town of Majahual on Tuesday, August 21, 2007. It was a Category 5 storm, with winds as high as 320 kilometers per hour. The high winds and water destroyed Majahual. Parts of Chetumal, 65 kilometers south, had floods. However, thanks to excellent preparations by the government and the people of Quintana Roo, not one life was lost on the Yucatán Peninsula.

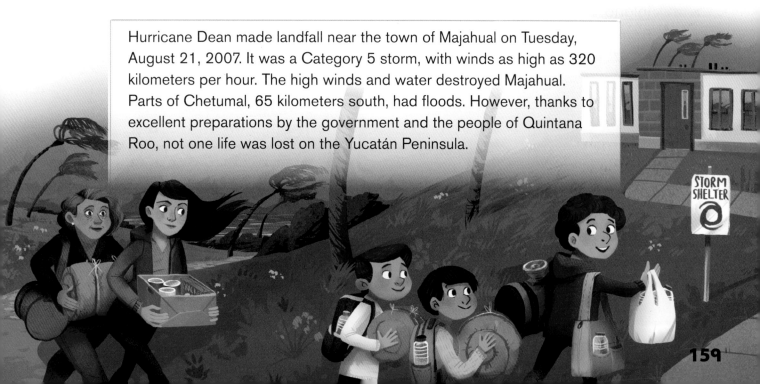

STORM SHELTER

Understand

Comprehension

Think How do you think the characters felt in the reading?
Would you feel the same way? Why or why not?

A Write each number in the correct place on the chart.

1 They are too young to help.
2 She is strong like her husband.
3 He stays calm even though he is young.
4 She is thankful that Luis's family can help.
5 He knows a lot about hurricanes.

Luis	
Luis's father	
Luis's mother	
Luis's brothers	1
Luis's aunt	

B Answer the questions.

1 What did the government learn from Hurricane Wilma?

_____

2 What did Luis do to prepare for the storm?

_____

3 Why did Luis's father ask Luis to prepare everything?

_____

C **Words in Context** Match each sentence to a picture.

1 The cars drove <u>inland</u>, away from the storm.

2 The high winds <u>destroyed</u> the old beach house.

3 The supplies were in the <u>trunk</u> of the car.

4 The hurricane made <u>landfall</u> on the island.

a

b

c

d

Grammar in Use

D Listen and read along. 🔊 3·25

> I've already made twelve sandwiches and four pizzas.

> Also, I've just put batteries in my flashlight.

> What is he doing? There isn't an emergency.

> He knows. He's just practicing. Plus, he loves to eat.

E Look at **D**. Are Jay's actions finished? Which action did he finish last?

F **Learn Grammar** Present Perfect with *Already*, *Just*, and *Yet*

You can use the present perfect with the adverbs **already**, **just**, and **yet**. These adverbs tell when something happened or didn't happen.

I've already packed everything.
I've just eaten dinner.
Have you cleaned your room yet? No, I haven't cleaned it yet.

already packed   *just* eaten   haven't cleaned *yet*

←——————+——————+——————+——————→
past   present   future

Complete each sentence with *already*, *just*, or *yet*.

1   Has Vince washed the car _____? It still looks dirty.

2   Don't worry! I've _____ packed the clothes. In fact, I did it yesterday.

3   Emma has _____ left for work. She left about a minute ago.

G Make a chart like the one below. Then talk to your partner about it.

> I've already eaten dinner.

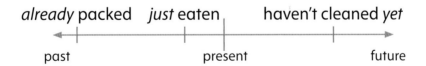

already done	just done	haven't done yet
eaten dinner	studied grammar	finished homework

Communicate

Listening

 Think How do you know if a storm is coming to your area?

A Listen. Match each force of nature to a safety tip. 🔊 3·26

1	Tornado ●	● **a**	Close all windows and doors.
2	Blizzard ●	● **b**	Go to the basement.
3	Severe storm ●	● **c**	Stay indoors and away from windows.
4	Sandstorm ●	● **d**	Keep blankets and food in your car.

B Listen again. Answer the questions. 🔊 3·27

1 How long will the tornado warning continue?

_____

2 How much snow may fall in Toronto?

_____

3 What may fall down during the severe storm?

_____

4 What should you carry outside during a sandstorm?

_____

Speaking 🔊 3·28

C Imagine a hurricane is coming. How will you prepare for it? What will you need? Discuss things you will need with your partner.

We need to get water bottles.

We also need …

I think we already have …

OK, what else … ?

We still need …

I'll get the …

Word Study

D **Learn** Phrasal Verbs with *Turn*

Some phrasal verbs begin with the verb **turn**.

They **turned** us **away** at the supermarket.

Listen and read the words. Then read the sentences and circle the correct phrasal verb. 🔊 3·29

turn on	turn back	turn in	turn up	turn over	turn down

1   When the boys **turned over** / **turned in** the rock, they found a sleeping lizard.

2   Mr. Garcia's students **turn down** / **turn in** their homework at the beginning of class.

3   The hikers went up the hill but **turned up** / **turned back** when it started to rain.

4   Lisa **turned up** / **turned down** the music after her parents said it was too loud.

5   Sue **turned on** / **turned down** her radio to listen to the news.

6   Allen **turned over** / **turned up** the television because he couldn't hear it well.

Writing Study

E **Learn** Adverbs of Manner

Adverbs of manner tell us how someone or something does an action. They are usually made by adding **-ly** to an adjective.

The waves were violent**. They smashed** violently **into the hotel.**
          adjective   adverb

Use the underlined words to complete the sentences.

1   He's a <u>careless</u> driver. He drives ____**carelessly**____ .

2   The trumpet is <u>loud</u>. Jack plays it very _____ .

3   The students are very <u>quiet</u>. They do their homework _____ .

4   Tim was very <u>brave</u>. He walked _____ up to the front door and knocked.

5   Annie's voice is <u>soft</u>. She always speaks _____ .

 Now practice writing in the **Workbook.** page 150

Wrap Up

Writing

A Read this how-to speech about preparing for an emergency.

Title — **Preparing Your Car for a Blizzard**

Greeting and Introduction — Good afternoon, everyone! Imagine that your family is in a car. Suddenly, your dad drives into a terrible blizzard. The car goes off the road. It's dark, it's cold, and you are stuck. How can you prepare for this? Let me explain four easy steps that may save your life someday.

Body with Steps and Order Words — First, always travel with a full tank of gasoline. If you get stuck, stay inside the car. With enough gasoline, you can start your car often to keep you warm.

Next, keep food and water in your car. Chocolate, cookies, and nuts can give you energy. Keep a can and matches in your car, too, so you can melt snow for extra water.

Also, keep coats, boots, and sleeping bags in your car. They will help you stay warm. Pack a flashlight and extra batteries so you can see inside the car at night.

Finally, always bring a cell phone so you can call for help. Be sure the phone's battery is always fully charged. On the phone, explain where you are. Road signs can give you important information.

Conclusion — These simple steps can save your life. Think about it. After a blizzard, do you want to build a snowman, or do you want to BE the snowman? Thank you!

B Answer the questions.

1 Why should you pack a flashlight and extra batteries?
2 Why should you take a cell phone when you are in a car?

Speech Tips
1 Greet everyone in your audience.
2 Make eye contact with people in the room.
3 Speak slowly, clearly, and with energy.
4 Thank your audience.

Learn Writing a How-to Speech

- Include a greeting and an introduction that gets your audience's attention.

- Organize your ideas on how to do something into steps. Use these steps in the body of your speech. Use order words, such as *first*, *next*, and *finally*.

- Include a conclusion with a strong, final thought.

 Write Now go to the **Workbook** to plan and write your own how-to speech. page 151

Project: Creating an Emergency Poster

C Create a poster that teaches someone how to prepare for an emergency.

- In your group, create a poster about preparing for emergencies.

- Think about the natural forces and emergencies you have learned about.

- Decide which emergency plan each person will create and what your group will include on your emergency poster.

- Design your emergency poster. Use pictures, drawings, and words.

- Practice explaining your emergency plan and a part of the poster. Write down any words that you want to remember.

- Present your poster and your emergency plans to the class. Make eye contact, use gestures, and speak clearly.

How should you prepare for a flood? First, be sure you know the quickest and safest way to get to high ground.

If there is a blizzard, will you be prepared? Make sure you have a lot of food and water in your house.

Emergency Supplies

Fresh Water

First Aid

Learn - Prepare - Stay Calm

?

BIG QUESTION 8

What can we learn from nature's power?

A Watch the video.

B Think more about the Big Question. What did you learn?

C Complete the **Big Question Chart.**

What did you learn about nature's power?

In units **17** and **18** you will:

WATCH
a video about biomes.

LEARN
about the importance of Earth's biomes.

READ
about Earth's biomes and a girl who explores one.

BIG QUESTION 9

Why are biomes important?

A Watch the video. ▶

B Look at the picture and talk about it.

1 What kinds of life do you see?

2 Where do you think this place is?

C Think and answer the questions.

1 How are parts of Earth different from each other?

2 What types of animals and plants live near you?

D Fill out the **Big Question Chart**.

What do you know about biomes? What do you want to know?

Get Ready

Words

A Listen and say the words. Then read and listen to the sentences. 🔊 3·30

| biome | desert | grassland | tropical rainforest | temperate forest |

| taiga | tundra | freshwater | equator | sloth | cactus |

1 Many plants and animals live in a **biome**.

2 The air in the **desert** is often cool at night.

3 The **grassland** is a perfect hiding place for a mouse.

4 Scientists have found new medicines in the **tropical rainforest**.

5 The **temperate forest** is full of colorful leaves in the autumn season.

6 The **taiga** has green trees and white snow in winter.

7 Be sure to bring warm boots when you hike in the **tundra**.

8 A river or lake is a **freshwater** biome.

9 It is usually warm and wet near the **equator**.

10 The **sloth** moved through the tree very slowly.

11 A **cactus** doesn't need water every day.

B Circle the correct answer.

1	It can be very hot near this part of the world.	tropical rainforest	tundra
2	You can find this in a very dry part of the world.	temperate forest	desert
3	This part of the world is usually cold.	grassland	taiga
4	Many farmers want to be near this biome.	desert	freshwater
5	This place has many trees.	temperate forest	grassland

C Complete the sentences with the following words.

| sloth   biome   cactus   equator |

A rainforest is a _____ near the _____. It's a good home for a
_____, but it's not a good home for a _____.

Before You Read

Think Which biomes do you live near? What are they like?

D **Learn** Classify and Categorize

Remember, you can **classify** and **categorize** information to help you understand it better. To categorize, gather pieces of information that are the same or almost the same into a group. To classify, give that group a name.

Read the paragraph. Categorize by putting the animals into groups. Animals can go into more than one group.

> Ocean and freshwater biomes are home to many kinds of fish. Ocean fish, such as the swordfish and the shark, can be very big. Whales in the ocean can be huge, but they are not fish. Freshwater fish, such as sunfish and freshwater trout, are usually smaller. However, the carp is a freshwater fish that can grow to be quite big.

whale	carp	swordfish	sunfish	shark	trout

Ocean Animal	Freshwater Animal	Big	Small	Not a Fish

E Now classify. What would be a good group name for *goldfish, redfish,* and *whitefish*? _____

F **Words in Context** Scan the article on pages 170–171 and circle these words. As you read, guess what the words mean.

> Arctic   hatches   glides   scenes

G Look at the pictures of biomes on the following two pages. How are the biomes similar and different?

Reading: Classify and Categorize **Unit 17** **169**

PREVIEW

The Natural Communities of Earth

In this *informational text*, you will read about Earth's biomes and the plants and animals that live together in these places. Remember, informational texts are true and give facts about real things. As you read, try to classify and categorize the information.

Earth Science

The Natural Communities of Earth

A polar bear hunts for seals in the Arctic winter. A baby eagle hatches from an egg high up in a forest tree. A sidewinder rattlesnake glides across the hot desert sand. What do these three scenes have in common? They are all examples of Earth's unique biomes. A biome is a community of plants and animals that live together in the same area. There are eight major biomes on Earth.

Aquatic Biomes

Oceans cover 75 percent of Earth, and many plants and animals fill this watery biome. Most of this ocean life lives near the surface, where there is sunlight and warm water. Near the coasts, coral reefs are part of this biome. Whales, dolphins, sea turtles, and many kinds of fish occupy the ocean.

Freshwater biomes include rivers and streams, ponds and lakes, and wetlands. Only three percent of all water on our planet is fresh water. Unlike ocean water, fresh water has less than one percent salt. Fish, frogs, and pelicans live in or near freshwater biomes.

Terrestrial Biomes

The **tropical rainforest** is a very important biome. Half of all the animal and plant species on Earth live there. Tropical rainforests are near the equator. Over two meters of rain fall there each year. The Amazon rainforest in South America is the largest tropical rainforest. Animals such as jaguars, spider monkeys, and sloths live there. Otters, which live near freshwater rivers and streams, are also part of this biome.

Think
What two biomes can the otter be in?

In **temperate forests**, new leaves grow on the trees in the spring. These leaves stay green until the autumn days arrive. Then they change color and fall to the ground. Squirrels, rabbits, deer, bears, and birds reside here. There are temperate forests in eastern North America, Europe, Russia, China, and Japan.

The **taiga** is a forest biome with evergreen trees. It is usually north of temperate forests. Winter days are short and cold, with lots of snow. Summer days are long and warm. Birds, beavers, moose, lynx, foxes, and wolves all dwell in the taiga. Large areas of this biome are in northern Canada and Russia.

Grasslands cover 25 percent of the land on Earth. They have rich soil and plants with deep roots. There are almost no trees in this biome. Because of this, people have turned many grasslands into farms. In Africa, grasslands are known as savannas. Gazelles, zebras, rhinoceroses, and many other animals roam these savannas.

Think

Which animal lives in both the temperate forest and the taiga?

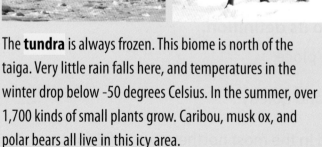

The **tundra** is always frozen. This biome is north of the taiga. Very little rain falls here, and temperatures in the winter drop below -50 degrees Celsius. In the summer, over 1,700 kinds of small plants grow. Caribou, musk ox, and polar bears all live in this icy area.

The **desert** is the driest biome on Earth. Less than 25 centimeters of rain fall each year. Plants that can live without much water, like the cactus, grow well here. Animals such as snakes and lizards also make their home in deserts.

Together, these eight biomes have provided a safe home for Earth's plants and animals for a very long time. By protecting our planet and its biomes, we can make sure that Earth's plants and animals continue to live in their natural, beautiful homes.

Understand

Comprehension

Think Tell your partner which biome you want to visit and three things you want to learn about that biome.

A Categorize the following animals into three groups. Classify by naming the groups.

~~polar bear~~ lizard frog caribou pelican snake

Tundra Animals
polar bears

B Circle True (T) or False (F).

1 Fish live in just one biome.   T   F

2 The desert gets very little rain.   T   F

3 Grasslands make good farms.   T   F

4 Fresh water is very salty.   T   F

5 The taiga is south of the tundra.   T   F

6 Most ocean life lives deep in the ocean.   T   F

C **Words in Context** Match each word to its definition.

1 Arctic   ●   ● **a** what you see in a place

2 hatches   ●   ● **b** moves smoothly and quietly

3 glides   ●   ● **c** the very cold land in the most northern part of Earth

4 scenes   ●   ● **d** comes out of an egg

Grammar in Use

D Listen and read along. 🔊 3·32

I've lived here since I was born. It's boring. I've dreamed about sailing on the ocean for a long time.

There are no pizza restaurants on the ocean, Jay.

Did I tell you how much I love this town?

We ♥

E Look at **D**. Which sentences tell about time?

F **Learn Grammar** Present Perfect with *For* and *Since*

Use the present perfect with **for** and **since** to show that something began in the past and is still happening now. Use **for** to talk about an amount of time.

These biomes have provided a home for animals for a long time.

Use **since** to talk about a specific point of time in the past.

I have studied biomes since February.

Circle the correct answer.

1 My dad has studied mammals **for** / **since** twenty years.

2 The government has protected this forest **for** / **since** 1998.

3 The butterflies have traveled to Mexico **for** / **since** centuries.

4 Scientists have lived in the Arctic **for** / **since** last year.

I've gone to school since I was four years old. I've gone to school for five years.

G Make a chart like the one below. Then talk to your partner about it.

Action	Since when?	For how long?
go to school	since I was four	for five years

Communicate

Listening

Think Which animals eat only plants? Which animals eat other animals?

A Listen. Write the words to complete the food chains. ◯ 3•33

| insects | ~~grass seeds~~ | hawks | lizards | coyotes | ~~shrub seeds~~ | snakes | quails |

Food Chain #1	Food Chain #2
shrub seeds	grass seeds

B Listen again. Answer the questions. ◯ 3•34

1 Where do plants get energy from? _____

2 What type of bird eats plants? _____

3 What type of bird eats animals? _____

Speaking ◯ 3•35

C What happens through the seasons? Talk about the changes.

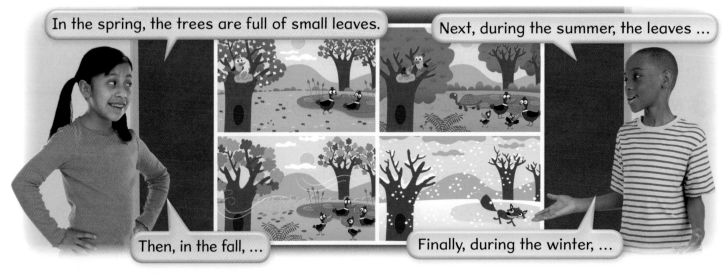

In the spring, the trees are full of small leaves.

Next, during the summer, the leaves …

Then, in the fall, …

Finally, during the winter, …

Word Study

D Learn | Words with -tch

The consonant combination **tch** sounds very similar to the **ch** sound, as in **chair**.

A baby eagle **hatches** from an egg high up in a forest tree.

Listen and read the words. Then write a sentence with each word in your notebook. 3·36

> **stitch   batch   itch   scratch   patch   catch**
> **A-Z**

Writing Study

E Learn | Complex Sentences with *Until*

Use **until** to connect two actions. The first action stops when the second action starts.

The cheetah ran until it caught the gazelle.

first action   second action

Circle the word *until* in each sentence. Underline the first action once. Underline the second action twice.

1   The scientist stayed in the desert (until) he ran out of food.

2   Rainforests will continue to disappear until we protect them.

3   The polar bear hunted for seals until it caught one.

4   Grizzly bears were in danger until people made a law against hunting them.

 Write Now practice writing in the **Workbook.** page 161

Vocabulary: Words with -tch • Writing: Complex Sentences with Until   **Unit 17   175**

BIG QUESTION 9

Why are biomes important?

Each biome is different and interesting.

There are unique plants and animals in each biome.

UNIT 18 — Get Ready

Words

A Listen and read the words. Listen again and say the words. 🔊 3·37

| parrot fish | seahorse | manta ray | sea turtle | marine park | snorkel |

| speedboat | border | petition | law | astonish |

B Write the words in the correct boxes.

> sea turtle   marine park   speedboat   border
> parrot fish   petition   seahorse   law   manta ray

Nature made this.	People made this.

C Answer the questions. Share your ideas with your partner.

1 What things in nature astonish you?
2 Would you like to snorkel? Why or why not?

Before You Read

 Think What places in your country are naturally beautiful? What can people see in these places?

D **Learn** Asking Open-ended Questions

Open-ended questions cannot be answered with *yes* or *no*. These questions ask for deeper answers and can help you understand a reading better. Open-ended questions often ask about your feelings and begin with **why**, **how**, **who**, or **what**.

Open-ended Question	Closed-ended Question
Why should people protect coral reefs?	Do coral reefs live in water?

Read the paragraph. Write open-ended questions about something you want to know more about.

Andrew snorkeled among the coral reefs every day of his vacation in Hawaii. He loved to watch the colorful fish there. He lost his goggles on the second day, so he had to buy new ones. One afternoon, Andrew saw a sea turtle in the water. He swam with the turtle until his father called to him from the beach. It was a very exciting day.

1 <u>Why did Andrew want to snorkel among the coral reefs?</u>

2 _____

3 _____

E **Words in Context** Scan the story on pages 178–179 and circle these words. As you read, guess what they mean.

> manage   invited   signed   difference

F Why should people protect Earth and keep it clean? Which parts of Earth do you want to protect? Why?

Camila's Journey

In this *realistic fiction* story, a girl named Camila visits a very special place and has a life-changing experience. Remember, realistic fiction has characters, problems, and settings that seem real. As you read, ask yourself open-ended questions.

★ **Belize City**

Camila's Journey

Camila lived in Belize City on the coast of Belize in Central America. Her father worked for the government's fisheries department, and he helped to manage the seven marine parks off the coast of the country. One day, Camila's father invited her to visit one of the parks with him.

"I'm going to Glover's Reef this weekend," he explained. "Would you like to join me?"

"Of course!" she said.

During their flight to the coastal town of Dangriga, Camila's father explained that Glover's Reef was on the edge of the Belize Barrier Reef, one of the largest coral reef systems in the world. Hundreds of fish and coral species lived in these reefs. He said that many coral reefs around the world were dying from pollution and overfishing.

From Dangriga, Camila and her father took a two-hour boat ride to Glover's Reef. Camila's excitement grew as they neared a small island with its beautiful coastline and turquoise water.

"We'll snorkel through the park tomorrow," her father said. The next morning, Camila and her father put on their goggles and entered the blue waters of the park. The beauty and variety of the underwater world astonished Camila. Hundreds of butterfly fish, parrot fish, and seahorses darted around her. She watched sea turtles and manta rays glide among the rainbow-colored coral. Camila saw how the plants and animals of the reef lived together perfectly. She took many pictures with her father's underwater camera. It was the most exciting experience of her life.

Think

Ask yourself an open-ended question about Camila's experience.

As they left the water, Camila and her father heard a loud noise. They turned and saw a large speedboat filled with tourists racing toward the reef area.

"They'll scare the fish!" shouted Camila.

"There's nothing we can do," said her father. "They're just outside of the park border."

Camila watched the boat continue along the border and then speed away. She was angry and upset.

At lunch, Camila was very quiet. When she finished eating, she turned to her father. "I'm going to do something for our planet's coral reefs," she said. "We need to help them."

Back in Belize City, Camila spoke to her class about coral reefs.

"In Glover's Reef, I learned that coral reefs are an important part of our ocean biome, because they are homes for hundreds of kinds of animals and plants. They are wonderful places to see the beauty of our oceans close up. My father taught me that coral reefs keep our shores safe from powerful waves, and that scientists can find new medicines from plants and animals that live there."

When she got home, Camila created a petition on the Internet. It read: *Governments of the world, please help the ocean's coral reefs. Keep our coral reefs safe and healthy for everyone.* In three weeks, 20,000 people in 38 countries signed Camila's petition. Within one year, three countries passed laws to protect their coral reefs.

"You have made a difference, Camila," said her father. "Thank you! The coral reefs of the world thank you, too."

Think

Ask yourself an open-ended question about helping coral reefs.

Think

Ask yourself an open-ended question about making a difference in the world.

179

Understand

Comprehension

 Think Would you do the same thing as Camila? Why or why not? Tell your partner your answer and reasons.

A Match each open-ended question to two possible answers.

1 How did Camila feel about the coral reef when she first saw it?

2 How did Camila feel about the boat and the people on it?

3 Why did Camila start a petition to help the planet's coral reefs?

a She felt it was beautiful and exciting.

b She wanted to protect them.

c She wanted to ask for people's help.

d She was very angry and upset.

e She was astonished by its variety of life.

f She didn't like what the people did.

B How did Camila help the world's coral reefs?

_____

_____

C **Words in Context** Circle the best ending to each sentence.

1 Camila's father helped to <u>manage</u> the seven marine parks,
   a so he told others what to do to keep the parks clean and safe.
   b so he went fishing in the parks every weekend.

2 When Camila's father <u>invited</u> her to go with him to the marine park,
   a he told her that she had to go with him.
   b he asked her if she wanted to go with him.

3 When 20,000 people <u>signed</u> Camila's petition,
   a they made a sign to put up in their school.
   b they put their names on the petition to show that they agreed.

4 When Camila's father said that Camila made a <u>difference</u>, it meant that
   a she changed something and made it better.
   b she could see how each coral reef was different.

PETITION

Grammar in Use

D Listen and sing along. **Speedboat, Speedboat** 🔊 3·39

Speedboat, speedboat,
You raced around the reef today.
You scared the parrot fish at play!
We've written a petition – stay away!

Speedboat, speedboat,
You raced across the reef today.
You chased around a manta ray!
We've signed a new law – stay away!

E Read the sentences. Which one tells when the action happened?

a You raced across the reef today.   **b** We've written a petition.

F **Learn Grammar** Present Perfect and Simple Past

Use the **present perfect** for past experiences, past actions that continue to the present, or actions that happened at an unspecific time.

Camila has created a petition. (We don't know when she did it.)

Use the **simple past** for completed actions that happened at a specific time.

When she got home, Camila created a petition. (We know when she did it.)

Circle the correct answer.

1 I **read** / **have read** this article about biomes.

2 They **snorkeled** / **have snorkeled** this morning.

3 He **went** / **has gone** to the Arctic last year.

4 The explorer **saw** / **has seen** a manta ray before.

> I have run in a race. I ran in a race last summer.

G Make a chart like below. Talk about it with your partner.

Action I have done	When I did it
run in a race	last summer

Grammar: Present Perfect and Simple Past **Unit 18** **181**

Communicate

Listening

 Think Which biome would you like to live in? Why?

A Listen. Match each name to a biome and a reason. 🔊 3·40

Name	Biome	Reason
1 Ricardo ●	● **a** tropical rainforest ●	● **e** see animals and hear birds
2 Sophie ●	● **b** tundra ●	● **f** see the leaves change color
3 Toru ●	● **c** temperate forest ●	● **g** sail around the world
4 Brigitte ●	● **d** ocean ●	● **h** take pictures of mountains

B Listen again. Then answer the questions. 🔊 3·41

Ricardo   Sophie   Toru   Brigitte

1 Who would like to see squirrels and rabbits? _____

2 Who would like to catch fresh fish to eat? _____

3 Who would like to live with native people? _____

4 Who would like to make friends with polar bears and seals? _____

Speaking 🔊 3·42

C **Learn** Asking About Needs

Use the verb **need** to ask about things that a person must have. The verb *need* can be followed by the word *for* (+ noun) or *to* (+ verb).

What do I need for my trip?
What do you need to wear?
What does she need to prepare?

Imagine you are taking a trip to a biome with your partner. Discuss what you will need.

We're going to the tundra. What will we need?

We'll need warm clothes and …

What will we need to do?

We'll need to …

Word Study

D **Learn** Words with the Suffixes *-ent* and *-ence.*

Some adjectives end in the suffix **-ent.** Often, these adjectives have a similar noun form that ends in the suffix **-ence.**

Camila looked at the different kinds of fish in the coral reef.
Camila made a big difference when she created the petition.

Listen and read the words. Circle the suffixes. Then write A for adjective or N for noun below each word. 3·43

| intellig(ent) | absence | independent | absent | independence | intelligence |

A-Z

__A__   _____   _____   _____   _____   _____

Writing Study

E **Learn** Complex Sentences with *Since* and *Because*

Use **since** and **because** to connect two actions. The action after *since* or *because* is the reason for the other action. *Since* or *because* can come at the beginning or in the middle of the sentence.

Since coral reefs are dying, we have to help them.
Because coral reefs are dying, we have to help them.

I want to live in the taiga since I like cool weather.
I want to live in the taiga because I like cool weather.

Circle the action that is the reason in each sentence. Underline the other action.

1   Since (rainforests have many plants and animals,) we must keep them safe.

2   Jason went to the marine park because his father works there.

3   Because the oceans are getting warmer, some coral reefs are dying.

4   Emma is going to the tundra since she wants to study the animal life there.

 Write Now practice writing in the **Workbook.** page 169

Wrap Up

Writing

A Read this fictional story about a boy who lives in the tundra.

Title —— **The First Catch**

Setting ——
Nanuq ate breakfast and got dressed. Outside the igloo, his father was packing the sled. Icy ground surrounded them for miles.

Dialogue ——
"We'll go to the water," his father said. "There are many fish there."

"How far is it, Father?" asked Nanuq.

"Maybe two miles, but don't worry. The sun will keep us warm."

Nanuq followed his father to the water. He watched his father dig a hole in the ice and wait. Many minutes passed. Then, his father pointed at the hole.

A large fish swam toward the hole. Very quietly, Nanuq's father held his spear and waited. Suddenly, he threw the spear forward and pulled out a large fish.

"You did it!" shouted Nanuq.

Nanuq's father gave him his spear. "Now it's your turn," he said.

Conflict ——
Nanuq was excited. He held the spear above the water and waited impatiently. When a fish appeared, he quickly threw the spear forward. He frowned as the fish swam away.

"Be patient," whispered his father. "You will know when it is time."

Solution ——
Nanuq watched a fish come near the hole. He waited a moment and then threw his spear forward. His father smiled as Nanuq pulled a huge fish out of the water.

Ending ——
Nanuq held the fish proudly. He would never forget this day!

B Answer the questions.

1 How would you describe the setting in this story?
2 How does Nanuq change by the end of the story?

Learn Fictional Story

- In the beginning, describe the setting to the reader. Use details to make the setting seem like a real place.

- Create interesting characters that use natural dialogue.

- Add a conflict, a solution, and an interesting ending.

 Write Now go to the **Workbook** to plan and write your own fictional story. page 170

Project: Acting in a Play

C **Create a play about a family that moves to a new biome. Then act it out.**

- In your group, discuss the biomes you have learned about. You will create a play about moving to a new biome.

- Imagine that your group is a family that will move to a new biome.

- Decide which biome you will move to, who will play each part, what each person will say, and how each person will act.

- Practice your play with your group and try to memorize most of what you will say.

- Write down any important words or phrases that you want to remember.

- Perform the play in front of the class. Act naturally, speak clearly, and have fun!

We're moving to the tropical rainforest! Let's start packing.

Doesn't it rain a lot there? I need to pack my rain jacket.

What will we do about all the insects? I'm scared of bugs.

We can study all the insects. I can't wait!

BIG QUESTION **9**

Why are biomes important?

A **Watch the video.**

B **Think more about the Big Question. What did you learn?**

C **Complete the Big Question Chart.**

What did you learn about biomes?

Definitions based on the *Oxford Basic American Dictionary for Learners of English.*

A

absence *noun* a time when a person or thing is not there

absent *adj.* not there

advertising *noun* the activity or business of telling people about things to buy

agriculture *noun* keeping animals and growing plants for food

antiques *noun* old things that are worth a lot of money

archaeologist *noun* a person who studies the past by looking at objects or parts of buildings that are found in the ground

architecture *noun* the design or style of a building or buildings

Arctic *noun* the very cold land and countries in the most northern part of the world

armor *noun* metal clothes that people wore long ago to cover their bodies when they were fighting

army *noun* a large group of soldiers who fight on land in a war

arrogance *noun* A person who has arrogance thinks that he or she is better and more important than other people.

arrogant *adj.* A person who is arrogant thinks that he or she is better and more important than other people.

arteries *noun* the tubes in your body that carry blood away from your heart to other parts of your body

ash *noun* the gray powder that is left after something has completely burned

assistant *noun* a person who helps someone in a more important position

asteroid *noun* any of the many small, rocky bodies that go around the sun

astonish *verb* to surprise someone very much

astronomer *noun* a person who studies or knows a lot about the sun, moon, planets, and stars

B

bacteria *noun* very small things that live in air, water, earth, plants, and animals. Some bacteria can make us sick.

banned *adj.* not allowed, or not allowed to happen

bark *noun* the hard surface of a tree

batch *noun* a group of things

batik *noun* (1) a way of printing patterns on cloth using wax on the parts that will not have any color (2) a piece of cloth printed in this way

batteries *noun* things that give electricity. You put batteries inside things like toys, radios, and cars to make them work.

battle *noun* a fight between armies in a war

beautiful *adj.* very pretty or attractive

biome *noun* all the plants and animals that live in a particular place, for example in a forest or desert

blizzard *noun* a very bad storm with snow and strong winds

blog *noun* a personal record that someone puts on their website saying what they do every day and what they think about things

blood *noun* the red liquid inside your body

bodies *noun* objects, such as those in space or on Earth. Moons and planets are bodies in space.

bodyguard *noun* a person or group of people whose job is to keep an important person safe

border *noun* a line along the edge of something

bottled water *noun* water that is sold in a bottle

brief *adj.* short or quick

brilliant *adj.* with a lot of light; very bright

broadcast *verb* to send out sound or pictures by radio or television

butter *noun* a soft yellow food that is made from milk. You put it on bread or use it in cooking.

C

cactus *noun* a plant with a lot of sharp points, which grows in hot, dry places

canal *noun* a path that is made through the land and filled with water so that boats can travel on it

canned food *noun* food that is kept in a can

canvas *noun* a strong, heavy cloth used for making bags, tents, and sails, or for painting pictures on

capillaries *noun* the smallest tubes in the body that carry blood

carbon dioxide *noun* a gas that has no color or smell that people and animals breathe out

carpenter *noun* a person whose job is to make things from wood

cartoonist *noun* a person who draws cartoons

cash *noun* money in coins and bills

castle *noun* a large, old building that was built in the past to keep people safe from attack

catch *verb* to take and hold something that is moving

ceiling *noun* the top part of the inside of a room

cell *noun* the smallest part of any living thing. All plants and animals are made up of cells.

cement *noun* a gray powder that becomes hard like stone when you mix it with water and leave it to dry.

century *noun* a period of 100 years

chemicals *noun* solid or liquid substances that scientists study and use

cinema *noun* (1) a movie theater (2) movies in general

cinnamon *noun* a brown powder that is used to give flavor to sweet foods

citizens *noun* people who belong to a country or a city

city council *noun* a group of people who make the laws of a city and help to govern it

city hall *noun* the government of a city and the offices it uses

clay *noun* a kind of heavy earth that becomes hard when it is dry

coax *verb* to persuade someone to do something by talking to them in a calm and gentle way

coffin *noun* a box that a dead person's body is put in

collapse *verb* to fall down suddenly

combines *verb* joins; mixes two or more things together

comet *noun* a mass of ice and dust that moves around the sun and looks like a bright star with a tail

commerce *noun* the business of buying and selling things

common cold *noun* an illness of the nose and throat. When you have a cold, you often cannot breathe through your nose and your throat hurts.

complex *adj.* difficult to understand because it has a lot of different parts

concentrate *verb* to give all your attention to something

congested *adj.* so full of something that nothing can move

contest *noun* a game or competition that people try to win

contrast *noun* a difference between things that you can see clearly

convenient *adj.* (1) useful, easy, or quick to do; not causing problems (2) near a place or easy to get to

conversation *noun* a talk between two or more people

core *noun* the central part of an object

corner *noun* a place where two lines, walls, or roads meet

corporate farm *noun* a large farm that is owned and run by a company

countless *adj.* very many

craters *noun* large holes in the ground, caused by something large hitting them

cyclist *noun* a person who rides a bicycle as a sport

D

dead *adj.* not alive now

decide *verb* to choose something after thinking about the possibilities

decrease *verb* to become smaller or less, or to make something smaller or less

dentist *noun* a person whose job is to take care of your teeth

desert *noun* a large, dry area of land with very few plants

destroyed *verb* broke something completely so that you cannot use it again

determine *verb* to discover the facts about something

diameter *noun* a straight line across a circle, through the center

diaphragm *noun* the muscle between your lungs and your stomach that helps you to breathe

dictionary *noun* a book that gives words from A to Z and explains what each word means

difference *noun* the way that people or things are not the same, or the way that someone or something has changed

dinosaur *noun* a big wild animal that lived a very long time ago

disability *noun* a physical or mental condition that means you cannot use a part of your body completely or easily, or that you cannot learn easily

discover *verb* to find or learn something for the first time

discuss *verb* to talk or write about something in a serious way

disease *noun* an illness of the body in humans, animals, or plants

dishonest *adj.* A person who is dishonest says things that are not true, steals, or cheats.

disk *noun* a round, flat object

disorganized *adj.* badly planned; not put in order

disprove *verb* to show that something is not true

dissatisfied *adj.* not pleased with something

distance *noun* how far it is from one place to another place

distrust *verb* to believe that you are not able to trust someone or something

donated *verb* gave something, especially money, to people who need it

drab *adj.* dull and not interesting or attractive

dream *noun* (1) something nice that you hope for (2) pictures or events that happen in your mind when you are asleep

dreary *adj.* dull, boring, or depressing

drop back *phrasal verb* to move into a position behind someone else, because you are moving more slowly

drop by *phrasal verb* to visit someone who does not know that you are coming

drop off *phrasal verb* (drop someone off) to stop your car so that someone can get out; (drop something off) to deliver something, often on the way to somewhere else

drop out *phrasal verb* to leave or stop doing something before you have finished

duplicate *verb* to make an exact copy of something

dwelled *verb* lived or stayed in a place

E

earthquake *noun* a sudden, strong shaking of the ground

editor *noun* a person whose job is to prepare or control a book or a newspaper before it is printed

eighty *adj.* 80

emergency *noun* a sudden, dangerous situation, when people need help quickly

emperor *noun* a man who rules a group of countries (called an empire)

entire *adj.* whole or complete

environment *noun* (1) [the environment] the air, water, land, animals, and plants around us (2) the conditions in which you live, work, etc.

equator *noun* the line on maps around the middle of the world. Countries near the equator are very hot.

equipment *noun* special things that you need for doing something

estimate *verb* to say how much you think something will cost, how big something is, or how long it will take to do something

exaggerate *verb* to say that something seems bigger, better, worse, etc., than it really is

examine *verb* to look carefully at something or someone

excavate *verb* to dig in the ground to look for old objects or buildings that have been buried for a long time

exhale *verb* to let air out of your body by breathing

exhibition *noun* an object or a group of objects that are arranged in a museum or another place so that people can look at them

exotic fruits *noun* fruits that seem strange or interesting because they are grown in other countries

expand *verb* to become bigger or to make something bigger

explore *verb* to travel around a new place to learn about it

export *verb* to sell things to another country

F

fair *adj.* treating people in an equal way or in the right way

famous *adj.* known by many people

farmer's market *noun* a place where farmers sell food directly to other people

fascination *noun* the state of being very attracted to and interested in someone or something

favorite *adj.* Your favorite person or thing is the one that you like more than any other.

first-aid kit *noun* a set of medical equipment that you use to help someone who is hurt before a doctor comes

flashlight *noun* a small electric light that you can carry

flood *noun* When there is a flood, a lot of water covers the land.

florist *noun* a person who owns or works in a store that sells flowers

fluid *noun* a substance that can flow; a liquid

food label *noun* information on the outside of a box, can, or bag that tells you about the food inside it

force *noun* power or strength

fragrance *noun* a nice smell

fragrant *adj.* having a nice smell

frame *noun* a thin piece of wood or metal around the edge of a picture, painting, window, mirror, etc.

freight *noun* things that trucks, ships, trains, and airplanes carry from one place to another

freshwater *adj.* not salty; not from the ocean

funnel *noun* a tube that is wide at the top to help you pour things into bottles

G

galaxy *noun* a very large group of stars and planets

garbage collectors *noun* people whose job is to take away the garbage from outside other people's homes

gather *verb* to bring together things that are in different places

generals *noun* very important officers in the army

geography *noun* the study of the earth and everything on it, such as mountains, rivers, land, and people

gifted *adj.* very intelligent, or having a strong natural ability

glides *verb* moves smoothly and quietly

graduate *verb* to successfully complete a high school, college, or university degree

grassland *noun* a large area of open land covered with wild grass

gravity *noun* the force that pulls everything toward the earth

grief *noun* great sadness, especially because of the death of someone you love

grocery stores *noun* stores that sell food and other small things for the home

H

haggle *verb* to argue with someone until you agree about the price of something

haircut *noun* (1) when someone cuts your hair (2) the way that your hair is cut

hatches *verb* When a baby bird, insect, or fish hatches, it comes out of an egg.

headline *noun* the words in big letters at the top of a newspaper story

heart *noun* the part of the body that makes the blood go around inside

hero *noun* a person who has done something brave or good

horizontally *adv.* in a way that goes from side to side, not up and down

huge *adj.* very big

hurricane *noun* a storm with very strong winds

I

ignorance *noun* lack of knowledge or information about something

ignorant *adj.* not knowing about something

ignore *verb* to know about someone or something, but to not do anything about it

immense *adj.* very big

immune *adj.* If you are immune to a disease, you cannot get it.

independence *noun* being free from another person, thing, or country

independent *adj.* not controlled by another person, thing, or country

infect *verb* to give a disease to someone

influenza *noun* an illness like a very bad cold that makes your body sore and hot

ingredients *noun* the things that you use when you make something to eat

inhale *verb* to take air into your body by breathing

inland *adj.* in or toward the middle of a country

inner *adj.* inside; toward or close to the center

intelligence *noun* the ability to think, learn, and understand quickly and well

intelligent *adj.* able to think, learn, and understand quickly and well

interview *noun* a meeting when someone asks you questions about a subject

introduce *verb* (1) to tell an audience the name of the person who is going to speak, perform, entertain, etc. (2) to make somebody begin to learn about something or do something for the first time

introduction *noun* (1) the act of telling two or more people each other's names for the first time (2) the first part of a book or a talk which gives an explanation of the rest of it

investigate *verb* to try to find out about something

invited *verb* asked someone to come to a party, to your house, etc.

itch *noun* the feeling on your skin that makes you want to rub or scratch it

J

jade *noun* a hard, green stone that is used for making jewelry

journalist *noun* a person whose job is to collect and report news for newspapers, television, etc.

K

kneel *verb* to bend your legs and rest on one or both of your knees

knight *noun* a soldier of a high level who rode a horse and fought for his king a long time ago

knit *verb* to make clothes from thick cotton or wool thread (called yarn) using special, long needles

knot *noun* a place where you have tied two pieces of rope, string, etc. together

knowledge *noun* what you know and understand about something

knuckle *noun* one of the parts where your fingers bend or where they join your hand

L

landfall *noun* (1) an arrival on land (2) the contact of a hurricane with a landmass

landscape *noun* everything you can see in an area of land

landslide *noun* a sudden fall of earth, rocks, etc., down the side of a mountain

latest *adj.* the newest or most recent

law *noun* (1) a rule of a country that says what people may or may not do (2) all the rules of a country

layer *noun* something flat that lies on another thing or that is between other things

leopard *noun* a wild animal like a big cat with yellow fur and dark spots. Leopards live in Africa and southern Asia.

live *adj.* to be or stay alive

local *adj.* describing a place near you

lungs *noun* the two parts inside your body that you use for breathing

M

magazine *noun* a kind of thin book with a paper cover that you can buy every week or every month. It has a lot of different stories and pictures inside.

major *adj.* very large, important, or serious

manage *verb* (1) to be in charge of someone or something (2) to do something that is difficult

mansion *noun* a very big house

manta ray *noun* a large, wide, flat fish with a long tail that lives in warm oceans

marine park *noun* an area of water that is protected by the government so that the animals and plants that live there can be safe from humans

mass media *noun* organizations, such as newspapers, television, and radio, that give information and news to large numbers of people

matter *noun* all physical substances, or a substance of a particular kind

mayor *noun* the leader of a group of people who control a city or town (called a council)

members *noun* people who are in a group

meteorite *noun* a piece of rock from space that hits the earth's surface

microscope *noun* a piece of equipment with special glass in it that makes very small things look much bigger

mistake *noun* something that you think or do that is wrong

moon *noun* (1) the big object that shines in the sky at night (2) an object like Earth's moon that moves around another planet

mucus *noun* a sticky substance that is produced in some parts of the body, especially the nose

N

navigate *verb* to use a map or some other method to find which way a ship or other vehicle should go

news conference *noun* a meeting where a famous or important person answers questions from news reporters

newspaper *noun* large pieces of paper with news, advertisements, and other things printed on them

newsreels *noun* short films of news that were shown in movie theaters in the past

niece *noun* the daughter of your brother or sister

O

observatory *noun* a building where scientists can watch the stars, the weather, etc., using special instruments

orbit *noun* the path of a planet or an object that is moving around another thing in space

organic food *noun* food that is grown or made in a natural way, without using chemicals

outer *adj.* on the outside; far from the center

P

package *verb* to wrap something or put something into a box before it is sold or sent somewhere

paintbrushes *noun* brushes that you use for painting

pale *adj.* with a light color; not strong or dark

paleontologist *noun* a person who studies very old, dead animals or plants as fossils

paralyze *verb* to make a person unable to move all or part of their body

parrot fish *noun* a type of fish with bright colors that lives in warm oceans. A parrot fish has a jaw that looks like a bird's beak.

pastels *noun* (1) soft colored chalk, used for drawing pictures (2) colors that are pale and not strong

pastime *noun* something that you like doing when you are not working

patch *noun* a small piece of something that is not the same as the other parts

peasant *noun* a poor person who lives in the country and works on a small piece of land

peel *verb* to take the skin off a fruit or vegetable

perspective *noun* the way of drawing that makes some objects seem farther away than others

petition *noun* a special letter from a group of people that asks for something

photographer *noun* a person who takes photographs, especially as a job

pianist *noun* a person who plays the piano

piece *noun* (1) a part of something (2) one single thing (3) a single work of art, music, etc.

plantation *noun* a piece of land where things like tea, cotton, or rubber grow

playground *noun* an outdoor area where children can play, especially at a school or in a park

port *noun* a city or town by the ocean, where ships arrive and leave

power lines *noun* thick wires that carry electricity

president *noun* (1) the leader of the country in many countries of the world (2) the person with the highest position in an organization or a company

pretty *adj.* nice to look at

printing press *noun* a machine that is used for printing books, newspapers, etc.

process *verb* to treat something, for example with chemicals, in order to keep it, change it, etc.

prodigy *noun* a person (especially a child) who is unusually good at something

publisher *noun* a person or company that prepares books, magazines, etc., to be printed and sold

pulse *noun* the beating of your heart that you feel in different parts of your body, especially in your wrist

pumps *verb* forces a gas or a liquid to go in a particular direction

R

radio station *noun* a company that broadcasts programs on the radio or on television

raindrop *noun* one drop of rain

ravine *noun* a small, deep, narrow valley

reins *noun* long, thin pieces of leather that a horse wears on its head so that the person riding it can control it

relief *noun* the good feeling you have when you are no longer worried or in pain

reporter *noun* a person who writes for a newspaper or speaks on the radio or television about things that have happened

rescue worker *noun* a person whose job is to save people from danger

ribbon *noun* a long, thin piece of material for tying things or making something look pretty

rickshaw *noun* a small, light vehicle with two wheels mostly used in some Asian countries to carry passengers. A rickshaw is pulled by someone walking or riding a bicycle.

S

scenes *noun* (1) places where something happened (2) parts of a play or movie (3) what you see in a place

scrape *noun* an injury or a mark caused by rubbing against something rough

scratch *verb* (1) to move your nails across your skin (2) to cut or make a mark on something with a sharp thing

sculptor *noun* a person who makes shapes from materials like stone, clay, or wood

seahorse *noun* a small ocean fish that swims in a vertical position and has a head that looks like the head of a horse

search *verb* to look carefully because you are trying to find someone or something

sea turtle *noun* a large animal with a hard, round shell on its back that lives in the ocean

sedimentary rock *noun* a type of rock formed from sand, stones, mud, etc., that settles at the bottom of lakes or other bodies of water

shading *noun* the use of color, pencil lines, etc., to create light and dark areas of a drawing or painting so it looks real

shapes *noun* what you see if you draw a line around different things; the forms of things

shrimp *noun* a small animal with a soft shell and a lot of legs that lives in the ocean. It turns pink when you cook it.

shrink *verb* to become smaller or to make something smaller

signed *verb* wrote your name in your own way on something

sketch *noun* a picture that you draw quickly

skull *noun* the bones in the head of a person or an animal

sleeping bag *noun* a big, warm bag that you sleep in when you go camping

sleigh *noun* a large vehicle with pieces of metal or wood instead of wheels that you sit in to move over snow. A sleigh is usually pulled by animals.

sloth *noun* a South American animal that lives in trees and moves very slowly

smartphone *noun* a cell phone that is able to do some of the things a computer can do

snorkel *verb* to swim underwater with a short tube that a person can use to breathe through

snowfall *noun* the snow that falls on one occasion, or the amount of snow that falls in a place

social network *noun* a website that allows you to connect with friends, family, and people who share your interests

solar system *noun* the sun and the planets that move around it

soldiers *noun* people in an army

souvenirs *noun* things that you keep to remember a place or a special event

space *noun* (1) a place that is big enough for someone or something to go into or onto (2) an empty place between things (3) the area outside Earth's atmosphere where all the other planets and stars are

spacecraft *noun* a vehicle that travels in space

space probe *noun* a spacecraft without people that collects information and sends it back to Earth

special *adj.* not usual or ordinary; important for a reason

speck *noun* a very small spot, mark, or piece of something

speech *noun* a talk that you give to a group of people

speechless *adj.* not able to speak, for example because you are shocked or very angry

speedboat *noun* a small, fast boat with an engine

spoil *verb* to become bad to eat or drink

squeezes *verb* (1) presses something hard (2) goes into a small space; pushes too much into a small space

stained *verb* left a dirty mark, which is difficult to remove, on something

stars *noun* the small, bright lights that you see in the sky at night

steamship *noun* a ship driven by steam

stitch *verb* to use a needle and thread to repair, join, or decorate pieces of cloth

storm shelter *noun* a place that protects people or animals from bad weather

storm shutters *noun* wooden or metal things that cover the outside of a window to protect it from bad weather

street painter *noun* a person who draws pictures on streets or sidewalks, usually with chalk

street vendor *noun* a person who sells things on a sidewalk or street, especially in a city

string *noun* very thin rope that you use for tying things

sugar cane *noun* a tall tropical plant with thick stems that sugar is made from

suit *noun* a set of clothing worn for a particular activity

supplies *noun* things that people need, such as food, medicine, or fuel

surface *noun* (1) the outside part of something (2) the top of water

swallowed *verb* made food or drink move down your throat from your mouth

system *noun* a group of things or parts that work together

T

taiga *noun* a forest that grows in wet ground in far northern parts of Earth

take after *phrasal verb* (take after someone) to be or look like an older member of your family

take apart *phrasal verb* (take something apart) to separate something into the different parts it is made of

take down *phrasal verb* (take something down) (1) to remove a structure by separating it into the pieces it is made of (2) to write something that someone says

take in *phrasal verb* (take something in) to understand what you see, hear, or read

take over *phrasal verb* to get control of something or responsibility for something

take up *phrasal verb* (take up something) to use or fill time or space

talented *adj.* having a natural ability to do something well

teamwork *noun* the ability of people to work together

telescope *noun* a long, round piece of equipment with special glass inside it. You look through it to make things that are far away appear bigger.

temperate forest *noun* a forest in a part of the world that is not very hot and not very cold

terrible *adj.* very bad

texture *noun* the way that something feels when you touch it

thief *noun* a person who steals something

three-dimensional *adj.* having length, width, and height

thunderstorm *noun* a storm with a lot of rain, thunder, and flashes of light (called lightning) in the sky

tomb *noun* a place that is often underground where a dead person's body is buried

tornado *noun* a violent storm with a very strong wind that blows in a circle

tourist *noun* a person who visits a place on vacation

trachea *noun* the tube in your throat that carries air to the lungs

treasure *noun* a collection of gold, silver, jewelry, or other things that are worth a lot of money

tripped *verb* hit your foot against something so that you fell or almost fell

tropical rainforest *noun* a forest in a hot part of the world where there is a lot of rain

trunk *noun* the part at the back of a car where you can put bags and boxes

tsunami *noun* a very large wave in the ocean, usually caused by the sudden strong shaking of the ground (called an earthquake)

tubes *noun* (1) long, thin pipes for liquid or gas (2) long, thin, soft containers with a hole and a covering (called a cap) at one end

tuna *noun* a large fish that lives in the ocean and that you can eat

tundra *noun* the large, flat, Arctic regions of northern Europe, Asia, and North America where no trees grow and where the soil below the surface of the ground is always frozen

turn back *phrasal verb* to return the same way that you came

turn down *phrasal verb* (turn something down) (1) to say "no" to what someone wants to do or to give you (2) to make something produce less sound or heat by moving a switch

turn in *phrasal verb* (turn something in) to give your work to a teacher

turn on *phrasal verb* (turn something on) to move the handle or switch that controls something so that it starts

turn over *phrasal verb* to move so that the other side is on top; to move something in this way

turn up *phrasal verb* (turn something up) to make something produce more sound or heat by moving a switch

U

uniform *noun* a special type of clothing that some people in the same job, team, etc., wear

unique *adj.* not like anyone or anything else

universe *noun* (the universe) Earth and all the stars, planets, and everything else in space

unusual *adj.* If something is unusual, it does not often happen or you do not often see it.

V

vanilla *noun* a substance from a plant that gives a taste to some sweet foods

varnish *noun* a clear paint with no color, which you put on something to make it shine

vast *adj.* very big

veil *noun* a piece of material that a woman puts over her head and face

veins *noun* the small tubes in your body that carry blood to the heart

vertically *adv.* in a way that goes straight up and down, not side to side

victim *noun* a person or thing that is hurt, damaged, or killed by someone or something

virus *noun* a living thing that is too small to see but can make you sick

volunteer *noun* a person who says that he or she will do a job without being forced or without being paid

W

washable *adj.* Something that is washable can be washed without being damaged.

(the) Web *noun* the system that makes it possible for you to see information from all over the world on your computer

website *noun* a place on the Internet that you can look at to find out information about something

weigh *verb* (1) to measure how heavy someone or something is using a machine (2) to have or show a certain weight

wheat *noun* a type of grain that can be made into flour

whole *adj.* complete; with no parts missing

whole food *noun* food that is considered healthy because it is in a simple form and does not contain any chemicals

worries *verb* feels that something bad will happen or has happened